Studies in Musical Genesis and Structure

General Editor: Lewis Lockwood, Harvard University

Studies in Musical Genesis and Structure

Anna Bolena and the Artistic Maturity of Gaetano Donizetti
Philip Gossett

Beethoven's Diabelli Variations
William Kinderman

Robert Schumann and the Study of Orchestral Composition

THE GENESIS OF THE FIRST SYMPHONY, OP. 38

JON W. FINSON

CLARENDON PRESS · OXFORD
1989

Oxford University Press, Walton Street, Oxford OX2 6DP

Oxford New York Toronto
Delhi Bombay Calcutta Madras Karachi
Petaling Jaya Singapore Hong Kong Tokyo
Nairobi Dar es Salaam Cape Town
Melbourne Auckland

and associated companies in
Berlin Ibadan

Oxford is a trade mark of Oxford University Press

Published in the United States
by Oxford University Press, New York

British Library Cataloguing in Publication Data
Finson, Jon W.
Robert Schuman and the study of orchestral
composition: the genesis of the First
Symphony, op 38.—(studies in musical
genesis and structure.
1. German music. Schuman, Robert, 1810–1856
I. Title   II. Series
780'.92'4
ISBN 0–19–313213–3

Library of Congress Cataloging in Publication Data
Finson, Jon W.
Robert Schumann and the study of orchestral composition: the
genesis of the First symphony, op. 38 | Jon W. Finson.
p. cm.—(Studies in musical genesis and structure)
Bibliography: p.   Includes index.
1. Schumann, Robert, 1810–1856. Symphonies, no. 1. op. 38, B flat
major.   I. Title.   II. Series.
ML410.S4F58 1989   785.1'1'0924—dc19   88–38236
ISBN 0–19–313213–3

Set by Oxford Text System

Printed and bound in Great Britain by
Biddles Ltd, Guildford and King's Lynn

to
E. Verne and Dorothy Drake Finson

Editor's Preface

Historical musicology has recently witnessed vigorous and wide-ranging efforts to deepen understanding of the means by which composers of various periods and traditions brought their works to realization. In part this trend has resulted from renewed and intensive study of the manuscript sources of works by many of the major figures in Western music history, especially those for whom new and authoritative complete editions are being undertaken. In part it has arisen from the desire to establish more cogent and precise claims about the formative background of individual works than could be accomplished by more general stylistic study. In many cases, the fortunate survival of much of the composer's working materials—sketches, drafts, composing scores, corrected copies, and the like—has stimulated this approach on a scale that no one could have imagined a century ago, when Gustav Nottebohm's pioneering studies of Beethoven's sketches and drafts first appeared.

This series provides a number of short monographs, each dealing with a single work by an important composer. The main focus will be on the genesis of the work from its known antecedent stages, so far as these can be determined from the sources; and in each case the genesis of the work will be connected to an analytical overview of the final version. Every monograph will be written by a specialist, and, apart from the general theme of the series, no artificial uniformity will be imposed. The individual character of both work and evidence, as well as the author's special viewpoint, will dictate differences in emphasis and treatment. Thus some of these studies may stress the combination of sketch evidence and analysis, while others may shift the emphasis to the position of the work within its genre and context. Although no such series could possibly aim at being comprehensive, it will deal with a representative number and variety of important works by composers of stature from Bach to Berg; perhaps earlier and later composers as well.

Jon Finson's study of the genesis of Robert Schumann's First Symphony (the 'Spring' Symphony), Opus 38, sheds valuable new light on this famous work, Schumann's first completed symphony. Focusing on sketches, drafts, and later revisions, Finson's narrative begins with Schumann's early and growing knowledge of recent symphonic tradition, chiefly Beethoven and Schubert; centres on the first completion of the 'Spring' Symphony in 1841; and then follows its subsequent revisions to the second and final version of 1852. He sets forth the growth of the work as we see it in Schumann's changes of content and orchestration, ranging from Schumann's initial burts of creativity in January 1841 (when the basic draft of the whole work was finished in four days) through the months of further work during that year; then to the later transformations over the next ten years and more. To his study of the surviving musical sources Finson adds vivid documentary evidence of the artistic context in which the young Schumann lived—chiefly the Leipzig of the 1840s, with its Gewandhaus Orchestra under his close friend Felix Mendelssohn. Reflected too is the background of musical opinion in these years—that of Robert and Clara Schumann and their contemporaries—on the problem of what composers in the wake of Beethoven and Schubert could still achieve in the genre of the symphony. Especially resonant for Schumann is the famous rediscovery of Schubert's 'Great C Major' Symphony. But the central focus is on the 'Spring' Symphony itself—its creative background and its significance for Schumann's first emergence as a symphonic composer.

Lewis Lockwood

Harvard University

Author's Note

Before beginning my discussion of Schumann's Op. 38, I should like to take a moment to acknowledge some of the authors who provided a foundation for this study, to outline one of its technical assumptions, and to recognize all those who directly supported my work on this topic. Like all scholars, I rely to a certain extent on my predecessors, and I should cite in this respect Georg Kinsky's work on Wilhelm Heyer's collection which provided the first detailed descriptions of the autograph sources for the Spring Symphony as well as Linda Correll Roesner's research on the mechanics of various sources as presented in her doctoral dissertation, in various lectures, and in private conversation.

My transcriptions of Schumann's autograph sketches (and score to a much lesser extent) represent unashamed reconstructions rather than diplomatic reproductions. My task in the ensuing study involves making sense of the composer's jottings, and it would be mechanical and uninformative (if not downright misleading) to reproduce them literally. Philip Gossett provides an excellent discussion of the problems with diplomatic transcriptions in his article, 'Beethoven's Sixth Symphony: Sketches for the First Movement', *Journal of the American Musicological Society*, xxvii (1974), 249, 280–4. Anyone interested in a mechanical reproduction of Schumann's sketches and score for Op. 38 may turn to the illustrations in this volume, to the widely distributed facsimile published by the Robert Owen Lehman Foundation, or to the many extant microfilms of the LC manuscript. Photographic facsimiles and microfilms are by nature imperfect, and for this reason I have checked all my transcriptions against the originals in the Library of Congress and revised them accordingly.

Finally, I wish to extend my deepest thanks to the many supporters of my research on Schumann's symphonies. Financial aid has been provided by the Martha Baird Rockefeller Fund for Music, the R. J. Reynolds Fund for Junior Faculty Development, and the University of North Carolina Faculty Council. A subvention for the printing of musical examples comes from the UNC College of Arts and Sciences, Endowment for Scholarly Publications, Artistic Exhibitions, and Performances, with special thanks to Dean Gillian T. Cell, Francis Whang, and Ann Woodward, Chairman of the Department of Music. The sources for the study have graciously been made available by Professor Asher Zlotnik; the Bonn University Library and I. Fischer, Oberbibliotheksrätin; by the Gesellschaft der Musikfreunde in Vienna and Otto Biba, archivist; by the Newberry Library, Chicago; and last, but certainly not least, by the Library of Congress and its staff, especially James Pruett, Head of the Music Division and Geraldine Ostrove, Head of Reader Services at the Music Division. For their encouragement and attention to the project, I should like to express particular gratitude to Bruce Phillips at Oxford University Press and Lewis Lockwood, Harvard University.

J.F.

Chapel Hill, North Carolina
January 1989

Contents

List of Tables

List of Illustrations

(between pp 118 and 119)

Key to Abbreviated Citations

AMZ	*Allgemeine Musikalische Zeitung* (Leipzig).
Briefverzeichnis	Schumann's ledger recording letters sent and received, Zwickau, Robert-Schumann-Haus, 4871 VII C, 10 A3.
Erler, *Briefe*	*Robert Schumann's Leben aus seinen Briefen geschildert*, ed. Hermann Erler, 2nd edn., 2 vols. (Berlin, 1887).
Haushaltbücher	*Haushaltbücher*, ed. Gerd Nauhaus, 2 parts (Leipzig, 1982).
Jansen, *Briefe*	*Robert Schumanns Briefe. Neue Folge*, ed. F. Gustav Jansen, 2nd edn., (Leipzig, 1904).
Jugendbriefe	*Jugendbriefe von Robert Schumann*, ed. Clara Schumann, 2nd edn. (Leipzig, 1886); index in Jansen, *Briefe*.
NZfM:	*Neue Zeitschrift für Musik* (Leipzig).
Tagebücher	*Tagebücher*, ed. Georg Eismann (Leipzig, 1971).

1 *Schumann's Preparations for Symphonic Composition*

From the time of its première Robert Schumann's First Symphony, Op. 38, has seemed the product of a Romantic creativity founded largely on inexplicable inspiration. An anonymous critic writing in the *Allgemeine Musikalische Zeitung* expresses just such a notion in one of the first reviews of the piece, applying it particularly to Schumann's orchestration:

Felix Mendelssohn-Bartholdy conducted the symphony by Robert Schumann that opened the second part of the concert by Klara [*sic*] Schumann; it went splendidly and justifiably received much applause. The symphony surprised us pleasantly in two ways: first in the intellectual and technical confidence with which it has been fashioned and developed, as well as in the natural style and above all in the manner of taste that predominate. Although Mr R. Schumann already has given well-known evidence of his fine talent in many compositions of smaller dimensions, like songs, piano pieces, etc., without anything further one could not infer the success of a larger work, an orchestral work at that. [Such a piece] assumes not only talent and proper musical training in general but also demands the necessarily more specialized acquaintance with the orchestral medium etc., that one can only attain through frequent practice, both in composition and performing. To our knowledge, however, this symphony is Mr Schumann's first orchestral work, and in this respect it deserves our fullest appreciation, for it is not only well and fluently written, but also, for the most part, knowledgeably, tastefully, and often quite successfully and effectively orchestrated.[1]

Schumann's arrival on the orchestral scene took his contemporaries by surprise because they had forgotten an episode in Leipzig's musical history: in April 1833 the Gewandhaus orchestra performed a movement from Schumann's unpublished G-minor Symphony with some success. Added to this experience were Schumann's years of studying other composers' symphonies

---

[1] '*Leipzig*. (Beschluss)', *AMZ* xliii (1841), col. 330; all translations are my own unless otherwise noted.

in his capacity as editor of the *Neue Zeitschrift für Musik*. A brief outline of Schumann's activity in the decade preceding the composition of the First Symphony reveals that its instrumentation, form, and content result from more than just mysterious intuition.

PRELIMINARY STUDIES IN SKETCHING AND ORCHESTRATION: THE G-MINOR SYMPHONY

Schumann's first experience with orchestration came at a young age, if we are to believe the brief autobiographical sketch he penned in 1840: 'I began early to compose; among other things, at the age of twelve [I set] Psalm 150 with orchestra, a few numbers of an opera, many songs.'[2] By the time Schumann had decided to become a professional musician (at the age of 20), his thoughts routinely turned to the composition of symphonies. He muses, for instance, in a youthful letter to his piano teacher, Friedrich Wieck, 'But do you know how [composition] pushes and pulls in me, and how I could have written symphonies numbering up to Op. 100, if only I had written them down . . .'.[3]

This statement might be dismissed entirely, were it not for a few short drafts of symphonic pieces in Schumann's early sketchbooks, including a 'Sinfonia per il Hamlet', probably an overture,[4] and the beginning of a symphony in E-flat major (Ex. 1.1). This latter sketch in Bonn University's *Schumann 15*, probably dating from the first part of 1832,[5] features a format Schumann would use in his orchestral drafts for the rest of his life. He arranges his adumbrations in systems of two staves, as if for piano, but various notations of specific instruments indicate an orchestral ensemble. The sketch displays a more complete

---

[2] Robert Schumann, *Selbstbiographische Notizen Faksimile*, ed. Martin Schoppe (Zwickau, n.d.), 3ʳ; Reinhard Kapp discusses this period in Schumann's life most intelligently, but like all other authors he is hindered by the paucity of documentation, *Studien zum Spätwerk Robert Schumanns* (Tutzing, 1984), 9–16.

[3] *Jugendbriefe*, p. 83.

[4] I have written briefly on this piece in 'Schumann and Shakespeare', *Mendelssohn and Schumann: Essays on Their Music and Its Context*, ed. Jon W. Finson and R. Larry Todd (Durham, NC, 1984), 130–3.

[5] The paper on which the draft is entered bears the same watermark (a stylized 'S') as some composition exercises done for Heinrich Dorn in 1832. See the discussion of *Schumann 16* below.

texture and harmonization than Schumann's later efforts; at this stage he probably composed at the piano and certainly thought in terms of the keyboard. None the less, the composer devised this draft in a musical idiom much more appropriate to symphonic than pianistic music: the harmonic rhythm is slow and would sound clumsy on the piano, in contrast to Schumann's deft idiomatic writing for the keyboard. And certain features, like the thematic working beginning in measure 31, would shine

Example 1.1   Schumann, excerpt from an unfinished sketch for a symphony in E-flat major, Bonn University Library, *Schumann 15*, p. 97

more brightly if the sketch were dressed in the robes of a fairly complex scoring. Schumann never used the opening measures of the draft, I suspect because they so resemble the head motive from the second movement of Beethoven's Ninth Symphony. (We shall see shortly how intimately Schumann knew Beethoven's symphonies and how he might come to have them on his mind.) The remaining, more original portion of this sketch yielded two ideas (mm. 31–7 and mm. 50–5) which Schumann retained for incorporation later in his G-minor Symphony (mm. 68–71 and mm. 235–44).[6]

Work on the G-minor Symphony, like Schumann's later activity with the *Neue Zeitschrift für Musik*, resulted from the increasingly severe paralysis of his right hand and the abandonment of his ambition to become a virtuosic pianist. Though the problem with his hand began earlier, perhaps as early as 1830,[7] Schumann did not seriously despair of his ability to pursue a pianistic career until June 1832,[8] when he finally broached the subject to his mother:

Eduard will have told you of the remarkable misfortune that has overtaken me. This is the reason for the trip to Dresden, which I want to make with Wieck next Monday. Although I am undertaking it on

---

[6] Measure numbers for the G-minor Symphony refer for the sake of convenience to Marc Andreae's conflated edition of the piece, *Sinfonie G-Moll für Orchester* (Frankfurt, New York, and London, 1972).

[7] The composer's entry in his diaries for 26 January 1830 reads, ' . . . mein betäubter Finger . . . ', *Tagebücher*, p. 222.

[8] Ibid. 410.

the advice of my doctor and also out of frustration, I am required none the less to work a good deal there.[9]

The composer tried various cures during the ensuing period, but he could not practise the piano, and he turned his energies to other constructive projects in the field of music.

Just a little more than a month after his traumatic announcement to his mother, Schumann wrote to his first music teacher, Johann Gottfried Kuntsch, about studying orchestration independently:

> I completed my theoretical courses up to the canon with Dorn some months ago; I studied Marpurg on my own. Marpurg is a very estimable theorist. Otherwise, Sebastian Bach's Well-Tempered Clavier is my primer, the best in any event. . . . Now I must turn to score-reading and instrumentation. Do you own any older scores, perhaps of old, Italian sacred music? About my plan I shall write to you later, if these lines do not remain unanswered by you.[10]

Schumann planned to compose a symphony, and whether or not Kuntsch sent his former pupil any Italian sacred music, we know that Schumann studied orchestral scores in order to learn instrumentation. We read later in the composer's diary during the incomplete work on the finale of the G-minor Symphony in 1833, 'Plans and tasks. Musical journal. To reduce the B-flat-major Symphony. Last movement of my symphony.'[11] Schumann refers to Beethoven's Fourth Symphony in B-flat major: we find a reduction of the slow movement in Bonn, *Schumann 16*, another of Schumann's contemporary sketchbooks.[12] Its initial pages contain exercises in counterpoint for Heinrich Dorn probably completed in April 1832.[13] The reduction for piano, four hands, begins on 6^r of *Schumann 16*, and the frequent notations about instrumental transpositions, melodic assignments, and doublings suggest that the reduction represents a study in orchestration rather than a mere transcription. Schumann would have had transcriptions of this symphony

---

[9] *Jugendbriefe*, p. 184.

[10] The letter is dated 27 July 1832, *Jugendbriefe*, p. 187.

[11] *Tagebücher*, p. 417.

[12] The book came from the Wiede collection; see Wolfgang Boetticher, *Robert Schumann: Einführung in Persönlichkeit und Werk* (Berlin, 1941), 640.

[13] *Jugendbriefe*, pp. 168–9.

available to him already, if he were only interested in playing it at the piano; he had no need to undertake such an exercise, unless he were following the age-old practice of reducing and copying in order to become intimately familiar with the details of structure and orchestration. Moreover, this reduction of Beethoven's Fourth Symphony is not an isolated example: after a set of variations for piano on a theme by Beethoven in *Schumann 16*,[14] we find a reduction for piano, four hands, of the 'third' Leonore Overture. Schumann is particularly concerned with Beethoven's manipulation of instrumental colour in this transcription, and we can find notes about transpositions of wind instruments, melodic assignments, doublings, and, on the second page (Illustration I), interplay between orchestral groups, 'Pauken, Trompeten, Hörner [deleted] und Posaunen schlagen vor, die anderen Blasinstrumenten nach'. Yet another example of Schumann's study of scoring by means of transcription is his incomplete version of the first movement from Beethoven's Ninth Symphony in the Deutsche Staatsbibliothek, Berlin (Mus. ms. 1256/40), which probably dates from this period. The notion that Schumann first sought to teach himself orchestration in all of these transcriptions seems consistent with the pride he expresses in his letter to Kuntsch about learning other fundamental musical skills by himself.

After Schumann had composed a substantial part of his G-minor Symphony in the summer and early autumn of 1832, he realized that he would require some outside help with his scoring. He availed himself of a second variety of instruction by seeking out the experienced conductor Christian Gottlob Müller, director of Leipzig's Euterpe Musical Society. The young composer wrote to Müller on 2 November 1832 when plans for the new undertaking already seem to have been quite advanced:

> The undersigned enquires of your Excellency whether you would be inclined to instruct him in instrumentation and humbly requests that for this purpose, you go through with him his own symphonic movement which will be played soon in Altenberg. How deeply you would find me in your debt I cannot say, for I have followed entirely my own instincts, without guidance, and lack, in addition, confidence in my symphonic talent.

[14] This piece has been published as Schumann's *Exercices. Etüden in Form freier Variationen über ein Thema von Beethoven*, ed. Robert Münster (Munich, 1976).

Any other conditions I leave to your good judgement.

I further request you to reply by return post at what time I could meet you at your home to discuss this further and to confirm a beginning . . .[15]

The letter also intimates the beginnings of Schumann's third strategy for learning orchestration: trial and error. Schumann arranged for a series of performances by relying on the good offices of his friends and supporters, and he then revised the work after each hearing. Kuntsch quite possibly helped to promote the performance in Altenberg near Zwickau, and Wieck may also have aided in arranging the concert, as Schumann's letter to his mother indirectly suggests on 6 November 1832:

How many happy things I have to tell you today! The first, that we shall surely see one another within fourteen days, occupied me the whole night long, so that I decided to get up in order to write and work—the second, that Wieck and Clara will be giving a concert near you—and the third, that a symphony by me will be played in [that concert]. May you find in this, my good Mother, the excuse for my long lapse in corresponding. I have been working continually for the past fourteen days, and I am anxious and doubtful whether I will be ready in time—I have given up my lodgings for two months (if you will have me that long), rented my piano to Lühe[16] during this period—in short, everything is ready for my departure except the symphony. . . . As far as my hand is concerned, the doctor is always consoling; *I, for my part, am fully resigned and regard it as incurable.* In Zwickau I want to take up the violoncello again (for which one only needs the left hand) which, moreover, is very useful in symphonic composition . . .[17]

This letter reinforces the thought that Schumann connected the composition of the symphony with his aborted career as pianist, that he intended to pursue his ambitions in this genre further, and it also suggests that he had a passing acquaintance with a stringed instrument, something he mentions nowhere else.

The first test of the symphony in Altenberg on 18 November 1833 brought mixed results. Wieck recorded in Clara's diary, 'First movement of Schumann's symphony was performed—but

[15] *Jugendbriefe*, pp. 192–3.
[16] Hans Eggert Willibald Lühe (1801–66), an author active in Leipzig at the time, who later bore the designation 'Juvenalis' in the *Davidsbund*.
[17] *Jugendbriefe*, pp. 193–4.

not understood. It also had too little of an effect—at least for
such a public—is well conceived and constructed—but too leanly
scored.'[18] Schumann copied a favourable review from a local
Zwickau critic in his diary:

The first composition for orchestra by Robert Schumann, a native of
Zwickau, formed a refined, beautiful part of this concert. He inten-
tionally gave the first movement its première in his home town, and
for this we, on our part, can only be grateful to him. The movement
is most artfully and ingeniously constructed from three melodies, and,
in fact, [is] very difficult none the less never superficial. . . . However,
one might desire a more strongly manned orchestra for this piece, the
Leipzig preferably, for which excellent musical ensemble above all [the
piece] may be warranted and appropriate.[19]

Whether Wieck's criticism about the scoring was just, or the
Altenberg orchestra lacked sufficient forces as the anonymous
reviewer suggested, Schumann felt the need to revise the
movement after he had heard it in concert. In a letter dated
17 December 1832 to the music publisher Hofmeister Schumann
writes from his family's home:

In my small, cosy, childhood room I am working industriously on the
symphony. To be sure, I often mistake yellow for blue in the
instrumentation of the first movement, but I consider this art so difficult
that only study may bring commanding certainty. If you could arrange
for it to be performed once this winter in Leipzig, that would be the
best encouragement for me. May this not sound presumptuous on my
part. You have always looked upon me with so much friendliness as
a disciple of art, that I believe I might venture such a request.[20]

Schumann not only sought the good offices of his Leipzig
publisher, but also any influence his family might bring to bear.
Shortly after he wrote to Hofmeister, he received an invitation
from music director Carl Cornelius Thierfelder to have his first
movement performed in Schneeberg, the site of the family
publishing business and home of his two brothers, Carl and
Julius. The composer replied to Thierfelder on 3 January 1833
in a letter which indicates that he was revising more than just
the instrumentation of the first movement:

I am very pleased by your invitation but regret that I can send

[18] *Tagebücher*, p. 472, n. 436.   [19] Ibid. 428.   [20] *Jugendbriefe*, p. 197.

neither the score nor the parts at the moment, because I have just completely reworked the first movement and have not copied the individual parts. When I first composed this movement, I really employed the rhythm

throughout; I resolved it only towards the end with the friendly and easier

For the Zwickau concert, I stayed with the latter throughout, and I have changed it in the new score to the older [version], not only because it is more fiery and unusual, but also [because it] has something contrary about it. You will hear for yourself and judge![21]

The concert in Schneeberg was first scheduled on 17 January but then postponed until 18 February,[22] and no account of its success or failure seems to remain.

Schumann's Leipzig friends had also prevailed on the Gewandhaus to perform the piece on 29 April 1833[23] in a concert again featuring Clara Wieck as soloist. Schumann wrote to his mother of this final performance, 'My symphony . . . has made me many friends among art connoisseurs such as Stegmayer, Pohlenz, Hauser. . . . You can well believe that I am busy with the many preparations for the paper [*Die Neue Zeitschrift für Musik*].'[24] And a reviewer commented in the *Leipziger Tageblatt*, '. . . Who would not have rejoiced in the . . . truly poetic and original Overture to a Midsummer Night's Dream by Felix Mendelssohn Bartholdy, and the imaginative symphony movement by Schumann.'[25]

We will see that the three-stage pattern of instrumentation first established for the G-minor Symphony persists for the orchestration of Op. 38. It involves the independent study of

[21] Jansen, *Briefe*, p. 38.
[22] See the *Jugendbriefe*, p. 201 for the initial date, and for the second date the composer's letter to Hofmeister in Jansen, *Briefe*, p. 414. Gerald Abraham suggests 12 February as the actual date of the performance; see his 'Schumann's *Jugendsinfonie* in G Minor', *Musical Quarterly*, xxxvii (1951), 48.
[23] Alfred Dörffel, *Geschichte der Gewandhausconcerte zu Leipzig vom 25. November 1781 bis 25. November 1881* (Leipzig, 1884), i. 209.
[24] *Jugendbriefe*, p. 212; the 'connoisseurs' mentioned were Ferdinand Stegmayer a Leipzig composer, Christian August Pohlenz music director of the Gewandhaus, and Franz Hauser a singer at the Leipzig opera.
[25] Dörffel, *Geschichte*, i. 209.

the orchestral repertory (in this case by reducing scores for piano), consultation with a resident conductor about the first draft, and a series of trial performances, each followed by more or less extensive revisions. In these last two stages, the composer often relied on a network of personal and professional acquaintances to secure the necessary renditions (even at this early date close ties emerge between Robert's premières of symphonic music and Clara's appearances as soloist). The knowledge Schumann lacked in his scant vocational training he gained from this empirical procedure.

The contents of the G-minor Symphony, its movements, themes, and formal arrangements, have long been known through articles and scores. The best account remains that by Gerald Abraham[26] and it requires no rehearsal here. We know considerably less about the autographs recording Schumann's progressive orchestrations because they remain in private possession, but it appears that the sequence of manuscripts[27] does present a progressive history of revision based on successive performances of the piece (see Table 1). With the exception of the Berlin fragment, these documents cannot be examined directly, but we can view Wiede 11/300a–d in photographs sold by an earlier owner to American Schumann scholar Asher Zlotnik. While we do not have Wiede 11/37 containing the first version of the initial movement, the working score of this section in Wiede 11/300b with its copious revisions displays two distinct layers: an intermediate version of the piece ostensibly deriving from 11/37 and a revised reading transferred to 11/300a. Because of its unique position, 11/300b gives enlightening evidence of Schumann's early technique of orchestration.

Schumann's scoring for the symphony, as it appears in the draft of 11/300b, reveals a fairly conservative instrumentation. Example 1.2a displays a page of this version with the ordering of parts Schumann would follow later for Op. 38: timpani at the top, trumpets and horns immediately beneath, followed by

[26] See Abraham, 'Jugendsinfonie', pp. 45–60; there is also an article by Egon Voss, 'Robert Schumanns Sinfonie in g-Moll', NZfM cxxxiii (1972), 312–19.

[27] The initial description of these documents from the Wiede Collection can be found in Boetticher, Einführung, p. 638. A catalogue of the collection can also be found at the Robert-Schumann-Haus, Zwickau; see Georg Eismann, 'Nachweis der internationalen Standorte von Notenautographen Robert Schumanns', Sammelbände der Robert-Schumann-Gesellschaft, ii (1966), 7–8.

TABLE 1. *Autograph sources for Schumann's G-minor Symphony*

Manuscript	Remarks
Wiede 11/37	Score of the first movement encompassing 478 measures, performed in Altenberg on 18 November 1832.
Wiede 11/300b	Transitional working revision of the first movement 492 measures long, including an incomplete score of the second movement.
Wiede 11/300a	Fair copy of the revised first movement 490 measures long, apparently copied from 11/300b and probably performed in Schneeberg on 18 February 1833 and in Leipzig on 29 April 1833.
Wiede 11/300c	Complete fair copy of the second movement, apparently copied from 11/300b, and an unidentified miscellaneous sketch.
Wiede 11/300d:	Partial score of the second movement, together with fragmentary drafts in score for the scherzo and sketches for the finale.
Deutsche Staatsbibliothek, Berlin, Mus. ms. 36:	One leaf of scoring from the beginning of the second movement.

the woodwinds, and finally the strings.[28] The trumpets still serve with the timpani to punctuate louder passages, and only two horns appear, reducing the options for combining melodic and harmonic writing afforded by the three or four instruments sometimes found in Beethoven. In this score Schumann recognizes the potential for added depth and variety afforded the lower strings by providing for separate cello and bass lines; this habitual division allows the cellos to pursue a melodic course while the basses provide a foundation. But in the G-minor Symphony Schumann only occasionally takes advantage of this division, and on the whole the intrumentation sounds more like that in use before 1800.

The distinct layers in 11/300b reveal a procedure which will

[28] See ch. 3 for a discussion of the rationale behind this ordering and its persistence in the composer's scores.

Example 1.2a   Schumann, G-minor Symphony, mvt. 1, excerpt from first layer of transitional autograph score, Wiede 11/300b

Example 1.2*b*   Schumann, G-minor Symphony, mvt. 1, excerpt from second layer of transitional autograph score, Wiede 11/300b

become familiar later in conjunction with Op. 38. In Ex. 1.2*a* from the exposition of the first movement the composer originally placed the melody in the first and second violins, later in the first clarinet (mm. 88–9), and then in the second violin alone (mm. 90–3). The accompaniment features the cellos and first bassoon in a contrapuntal role with syncopated violas displacing the same line by an eighth note; the basses doubled by a single horn and sometimes the second bassoon sound a pedal B flat. In the revised second layer of this section (Ex. 1.2*b*) Schumann tends to reinforce the melodic lines: the flute doubles the violins in measures 86 to 88 and the first horn helps the second violins in measures 92 to 93. He replaces the syncopated figures in the viola with a more straightforward rhythmic doubling of the cellos and first bassoon, he deletes the horn pedal, and he adds the second horn at the end of the excerpt to aid with the desired crescendo. Schumann tends to score the melody lightly in the first layer of Wiede 11/300b, and at the same time he seems to prefer intricate accompanimental patterns and doublings which interfere with the clarity of the texture. His revised instrumentation for the symphony reinforces the melody and reduces complexity in the accompaniment where it obscures more important lines.

Just this brief outline of Schumann's experience with his early symphony shows that he had begun to study and practise many of the skills necessary for orchestral composition before the composition of Op. 38. His abandonment of the successful G-minor Symphony might seem somewhat curious, but the founding of the *Neue Zeitschrift* occupied his imagination during mid-1833, and a fight for control of the journal made increasing demands on his time.[29] We should not be too surprised that Schumann spent his remaining hours writing for the piano, the instrument that had earlier formed the focus of his virtuosic aspirations. Reinhard Kapp may be correct in suggesting that Schumann composes in an orchestral style for piano during the decade of the 1830s, and that his music from this period determines his later aural image of instrumental ensembles.[30] Schumann's early works for piano certainly feature the same full

---

[29] See Leon B. Plantinga, *Schumann as Critic* (New Haven and London, 1967), 9–15.
[30] Kapp, *Spätwerk*, pp. 38–75.

texture found in his later symphonic pieces, reflecting a preference for voluptuous sonorities heard frequently in the composer's output as a whole. But whatever the connection between Schumann's early pianistic and later orchestral sonorities, his most direct and intense preoccupation with orchestral music after the G-minor Symphony comes in the context of the *Neue Zeitschrift*. Just as the G-minor Symphony provides Schumann with an autodidactic course in orchestral composition, reviewing other composer's work affords him an opportunity for another variety of self-instruction.

SCHUMANN'S CRITICISM AND HIS CONCEPT OF SYMPHONIC 'PROGRESS'

From his activity as a critic Schumann learned more about the orchestra as an institution, about the mechanism for publishing symphonic music in Leipzig, and about the course modern composers might chart for the future of the symphony as a genre. We cannot view the whole scope of the critic's concerns about the orchestral literature here, but we can highlight in passing the writings on orchestral performance and the underlying tenets of the symphony most relevant to the compositional history of Op. 38. Schumann would naturally focus much of his critical attention on orchestral music, inasmuch as the Gewandhaus was the most distinguished musical institution in the city. The arrival of Felix Mendelssohn shortly after Schumann gained full control of the *Neue Zeitschrift* increased the critic's enthusiasm for the Gewandhaus.[31] Schumann's writing about the orchestra is distinguished by his attention to the details of its organization and inner workings:

Before we say farewell to the Gewandhaus concerts for half a year, we would like to bestow a wreath of honour upon the forty to fifty members of the orchestra. We have no soloists like Brod in Paris or Harper in London; but these cities could scarcely boast of such ensemble at the symphony. And this lies simply in the nature of relationships. Musicians here form a family whose [members] see one another daily and practise daily; [the players] are always the same, so that they could

[31] For Schumann's initial reaction, see 'Schwärmbriefe. Eusebius an Chiara.', *NZfM* iii (1835), 126–7.

probably play Beethoven's symphonies without the parts. [Add] to this a concertmaster who knows the scores to the latter by heart and a director who knows them backward and forward—and the wreath of honour is complete. I would wish to give one leaf in particular to the timpanist of the orchestra (Hrn. Pfund [sic]), who is always there and ready like thunder and lightning; he plays splendidly.[32]

Normally a critic would be concerned with the quality of an orchestra's execution in concert, but Schumann chooses to comment on the rehearsal habits at the Gewandhaus and the orchestra's close relationship to its conductor and concertmaster. Schumann must have contemplated the uses he might make of the diligence and perfectionism at practice sessions under Mendelssohn's leadership.

Schumann also takes a keen interest in the workings of the all-instrumental Euterpe Music Society, whose meetings offered still more opportunities for presenting orchestral literature. His ear for detailed perception of orchestral playing could be acute:

The performance of symphonies and overtures [at the Euterpe] is not much inferior to those at the Gewandhaus concerts, since the musicians mostly come from there. If one plays with more respect there, one plays more vigorously here; if the director there holds the tempo as solid as a rock, a Beethoven scherzo goes head over heels to the end here. Both institutions are useful to one another, both [exert] the greatest influence on the various [musical] estates of their listeners. Certain mistakes should never occur, of course, and deserve some sort of capital punishment. For instance, an Euterpist blew a damnable C-sharp in the first beats of the Allegretto from the Seventh Symphony by Beethoven; but we want to attribute such cases to a teasing gremlin, who happened, just this once, to crawl into the oboe bore.[33]

In the course of both Gewandhaus and Euterpe concerts Schumann not only observed the interactions and potential of the ensembles, he also heard a great number of symphonies, and he read even more in his position as critic. His keen interest in the genre is reflected by the fact that he reserved to himself the right to review important orchestral works. The literature as reflected in reviews would be largely familiar to modern

---

[32] 'Rückblick auf das Leipziger Musikleben im Winter 1837–1838', NZfM viii (1838), 115.
[33] 'Fragmente aus Leipzig', NZfM vi (1837), 209.

audiences. Then, as now, works by Haydn, Mozart, and Beethoven formed the basis of orchestral repertory, but many works by unfamiliar composers appeared in concert and print, including symphonies by Onslow, Méhul, Kalliwoda, Spohr, and Müller. As a critic, Schumann felt obliged to pay particular attention to new symphonies[34] which he weighed against a set of criteria conditioned by his notion of the genre's tradition. He expresses these expectations most clearly in an 1839 review of composers we have almost forgotten since, Gottfried Preyer, Carl Gottlieb Reißiger, and Franz Lachner. At the opening of the essay written just eighteen months before he began work on Op. 38 the composer summarizes almost a decade of experience attending orchestral concerts and reviewing scores in Leipzig:

When a German speaks of symphonies, he speaks of Beethoven: he considers the two words as one and indivisible; they are his pride and joy. Just as the Italian has Naples, the Frenchman has the Revolution, and the Englishman his merchant marine, so the German has his Beethoven symphonies. Because of Beethoven he forgets that he cannot boast of a great school of painters, and he wins in spirit the many battles forfeited to Napoleon. He may even dare to place Beethoven on the same plane as Shakespeare. Now that the creations of this master have been grafted into our innermost beings—some of the symphonic [pieces] have even become popular—one would think that they had left deep marks behind them which would be exhibited by works in the same genre during the ensuing period. This is not so. We do find reminiscences—peculiarly, though, only of the earlier symphonies of Beethoven, as if each one needed a certain period before it could be understood—reminiscences too frequent and too strong; only rarely do we find continuation or command of this magnificent form, where measure after measure the ideas appear to change but are connected by an inner spiritual bond. The most recent symphonies lapse into the style of overtures, particularly the first movements; the slow ones are only there because they may not be omitted; the scherzos bear only the name; the final movements no longer recall what the previous ones contained.[35]

---

[34] He devotes one or two major articles every year to symphonic literature as well as a host of lesser pieces in the *Neue Zeitschrift*, usually writing them himself. Besides his review of Berlioz's *Symphonie fantastique*, the longer essays include 'Die Preissymphonie', *NZfM*, v (1836), 147–8, 151–2; 'Symphonieen', *NZfM* vii (1837), 111–12; 'Concertouverturen für Orchester', *NZfM* x (1839), 185–7; 'Neue Symphonieen für Orchester', *NZfM* xi (1839), 1–3, 17–18.

[35] 'Neue Symphonieen für Orchester', p. 1.

These remarks display what Plantinga calls Schumann's 'deterministic view of history in which a central tradition in music could be expected to develop in certain orderly and predictable ways'.[36] The basic tradition of the symphony in the critic's conceptual scheme proceeded not from Beethoven's style but from his construction of a musical fabric connecting the various movements by means of motives or longer melodic cells as well as by means of underlying tonal references. This melodic–harmonic interweaving—what I shall call the symphonic web—constituted in the critic's opinion the *sine qua non* of the symphony, but it provided only a foundation. Progress built on this foundation meant discarding the Beethovenian surface (the 'reminiscences too frequent and too strong' of the kind which found their way into the sketches like Ex. 1.1 of the young Schumann) and inventing a new symphonic idiom.

The creation of a fresh and modern orchestral speech proved a formidable task, and by the time of the 1839 review all of Schumann's listening and reading had produced only two composers who he felt were capable of continuing the 'magnificent' symphonic tradition:

A phenomenon was proclaimed to us in *Berlioz*. Germans in general know next to nothing about him; what has been spread about by hearsay seems rather to repel Germans, and thus a bit of time will probably pass before they become acquainted with him thoroughly. Certainly, however, he will not have laboured in vain; no manifestation appears in a vacuum. The immediate future will teach us this. *Franz Schubert* might also be mentioned; but his accomplishments in the area of the symphony have not yet become public.[37]

Schumann's comments on Berlioz betray the mixed opinion that had marked the critic's first encounter with the *Symphonie fantastique*. He could easily read the evidence of the composer's ability to create the symphonic web in gestures like the *idée fixe*, and he had no doubt that Berlioz had created a novel symphonic idiom. In fact, Berlioz was so inventive, his musical language so unprecedented, that it raised the question of his technical competence. In his apologia for the first movement Schumann

[36] Leon B. Plantinga, 'Schumann's Critical Reaction to Mendelssohn', *Mendelssohn and Schumann: Essays on Their Music and Its Context*, ed. Jon W. Finson and R. Larry Todd (Durham, NC, 1984), 17.
[37] 'Neue Symphonieen für Orchester', p. 1.

reveals his concept of symphonic form and something of his expectations for progress in formal matters:

[I aim] to demonstrate to those who know the work but fail to appreciate it that, despite its apparent formlessness, a symmetrically ordered pattern governs its larger proportions—not to mention the inner consistency of the movements. But the unfamiliarity of this new form, of this new mode of expression, is bound to lead to unfortunate misunderstanding. Most listeners fasten too strongly onto details at first or second hearing. The same thing happens when we read a difficult handwriting: if, while deciphering it, we pause over each individual word, we need disproportionately more time than if we first scan the whole passage for its meaning and purpose. Besides, as I have already suggested, nothing arouses disagreement and opposition so quickly as a new form bearing an old name. . . .

If we now try to comprehend the first Allegro in its entirety as an extended arch, without being disturbed by small, though to be sure, often sharply projecting corners, this form becomes clear:

First theme
(G major)

Middle sections   Middle Sections
with a second   with a second
theme   theme

First theme   First theme
(C major) .... (C major)
Beginning   Close
(C major) . . . (G major, E minor) . . . (E minor, G major) . . . (C major)

This we can compare with the traditional model:

Middle section
(A minor)
(Development of
both themes)

Second theme   First theme
(G major)...................(C major)

First Theme   Second theme
(C major)   (C major)

We could not guess what advantages of unity or variety the second form is supposed to have over the first; but let us say in passing that we wish we too possessed such an enormous imagination and could just let go![38]

[38] Robert Schumann, ' "Aus dem Leben eines Künstlers" [etc.]', *NZfM* iii (1835), 37–8; I have adapted this translation from Edward T. Cone's edition, Hector Berlioz, *Fantastic Symphony* (New York, 1971), 230–1.

Schumann's concept of sonata-form here—and by extension, of all formal matters—essentially constitutes an abstraction derived from generalizations about traditional examples. (In this sense Schumann's thinking already contains a strong, if somewhat latent, element of neo-classicism.) When a composer wishes for some formal novelty in one of the traditional genres, he rearranges the components of the abstraction, much as an architect would move elements in a blueprint. Architectonic structure in Schumann's view therefore takes on an almost mechanical aspect.

Although Berlioz can deal successfully with architectonic form, spin the symphonic web, and produce a fresh orchestral idiom, Schumann none the less finds much of the composer's more flamboyant musical language graceless. The intensity of this objection grows at the end of the 1830s as the critic becomes familiar with full scores of Berlioz's music; he expresses many misgivings in an 1839 review of the *Grande Ouverture de Waverley*:

In short, Berlioz's music must be heard; looking at the score will not suffice in itself, and similarly, one might try in vain to make sense of it at the piano. Often there are merely effects of texture and sonority, idiosyncratic chord-clusters inserted for support, often remarkable façades which even the practised ear cannot realize clearly according to the mere appearance of the notes on paper. If one traces the individual ideas to their roots, they often seem common, even trivial, taken by themselves. The whole, however, exerts an irresistible charm on me, in spite of much which is painful and unfamiliar to the German ear. Berlioz reveals himself differently in each of his works, ventures in each into another region; one does not know whether to call him a genius or a shameless huckster: like a bolt of lightning he illuminates, but he leaves the smell of brimstone behind him; he sets down great statements and truths, and then, suddenly, indulges in childish babbling.[39]

In the final event, Schumann cannot accept the rough surface of Berlioz's music. When chided for his neglect of the composer's 1843 concert in Leipzig, Schumann merely comments:

At present, I confess, I should be harsher with much of his work [harsher, that is, than in the *Symphonie fantastique* review]. The years make one more severe, and the unlovely things I found in Berlioz's

---

[39] 'Concertouverturen für Orchester', p. 187; I have adapted part of this translation from Plantinga, *Schumann as Critic*, p. 248.

early music (and I think I pointed them out then) have become no more beautiful in the interim.[40]

Schumann does not confess in this review his other reason for quietly forsaking Berlioz's symphonic idiom: Leipzig audiences exhibited no enthusiasm for the French composer's writing. Mendelssohn did not support Berlioz's cause, and the small Gewandhaus orchestra in its normal state was entirely unsuited to the composer's demands, as he plainly observes in his account of his tour of the city in 1843.[41]

In his 1839 review Schumann mentioned Franz Schubert, in cryptic terms intimating undisclosed information, as his second candidate for the creation of a new orchestral idiom. He had in mind the unpublished C-major Symphony which had already been heard in Leipzig while he had been in Vienna. The first thing Schumann observed about the piece concerned the process by which it came to press in Leipzig: he acted initially as an agent for Ferdinand Schubert who had called his attention to the manuscript. Schumann wrote to Raimund Härtel on 6 January 1839 about the various unpublished properties in Schubert's estate, and on 12 January Härtel requested a symphony, saying that a performance could be arranged in Leipzig that season. Ferdinand Schubert forwarded copies of two scores through Diabelli & Co. at the end of January, and Mendelssohn, who had been alerted, scheduled a performance of one selection at the Gewandhaus on 21 March 1839. Härtel then filed a report with Schumann:

Yesterday the Schubert Symphony (the one that arrived without the parts) was given in the last subscription concert, and although voices here and there were raised against its length, for it lasts a good hour, yet it has pleased. Accordingly, we are inclined to engrave it, and ask you, since you once interested yourself in the affair, to speak to Herr Schubert, if you please, in our name.[42]

---

[40] Plantinga, *Schumann as Critic*, p. 249.

[41] A colourful account of the composer's experiences with the orchestra in Leipzig can be found in *Memoirs of Hector Berlioz, Member of the French Institute, including his travels in Italy, Germany, Russia and England, 1803–1865*, trans. David Cairns (New York, 1969), 295–9.

[42] Otto Erich Deutsch provides a good account of the events surrounding the publication in 'The Discovery of Schubert's Great C-Major Symphony: A Story in Fifteen Letters', *Musical Quarterly*, xxxviii (1952), 528–33; I provide only a brief summary of the history here and I have adapted the translations from the article.

Schumann observed that Mendelssohn played the pivotal role in such matters, because he directed the Gewandhaus, selected its repertory, and influenced the Härtels, two of whom sat on the orchestra's board of directors.[43] The conductor wrote to Ferdinand Schubert after the performance:

You have given us all a great, lively pleasure by sending both symphonies by your brother. They arrived here so late that it was only possible to perform one of them, since only the last of our subscription concerts remained, and since the Symphony No. 7, which you sent only in score, seemed to me quite extraordinarily distinguished (and I rather thought that it would have more appeal here than the other), I had it quickly copied, and we performed it at the final concert, last Thursday, the 21st, to general, quite hearty applause. Each movement was followed by long and loud applause and, even more significant, all the musicians in the orchestra were deeply stirred and overjoyed by the admirable work. It has had more success than most of the other newer things from the last four years, and we shall repeat it at the beginning of the next concert season.[44]

Mendelssohn's devotion to Schubert's piece ensured a good performance and, in turn, a favourable public reception. And Leipzig publishers looked for this public approval before assuming the risk of printing a symphony in orchestral form (as opposed to the mere piano reduction accorded to pieces like the *Symphonie fantasique*). Schumann must have noticed that this series of events coincided nicely with his youthful preference for testing his orchestration at actual performances. If Mendelssohn could be persuaded to advocate a Schumann symphony, using the meticulously trained Gewandhaus orchestra, the composer would gain a trial rehearsal of his own instrumentation, a première to test the effect of the piece on the audience, and a hearing before Leipzig's active musical press, all at the same time.

Schumann waited for the appearance of the printed score of Schubert's new symphony to reveal his reaction to the music itself. In his review of 10 March 1840 (just six months before he would again turn his attention to symphonic sketching) he stresses Schubert's autonomy from the Beethovenian style. The Great C-major Symphony represents progress:

43 Dörffel, *Geschichte*, i. 233.
44 Deutsch, 'The Discovery', pp. 529–30.

It is often said to the dismay of composers, 'after Beethoven, better to abstain from symphonic spheres', and it is partly true that, apart from a few isolated, significant orchestral works more indicative of their composers' progress than influential among the general public, most pieces were lustreless reflections of the Beethovenian manner, not to mention those lame, boring symphony-makers capable of imitating the wig and powder of Haydn and Mozart without imitating the heads underneath. Berlioz belongs to France and is considered, at the moment, an interesting foreigner and eccentric. I had always hoped, and so many with me, no doubt, that Schubert, who had proved himself so firm in command of form, so inventive, so versatile in other genres, would turn to the symphony and leave his mark on it, and through it, on the general public; this hope has now been fulfilled in the most magnificent way.[45]

Schumann repeatedly touches on Schubert's new style, extending his comments to almost all aspects of symphonic construction. The critic ironically views Schubert's willingness to deal within the established outlines of conventional architectonics as a refreshing change:

The complete independence of the symphony from those of Beethoven is another sign of its mature origins [*ihres männlichen Ursprungs*]. Here one sees how correctly and wisely Schubert's genius reveals itself. Conscious of his more modest abilities, he avoids imitating the audacious relationships and the grotesque forms we encounter in Beethoven's later works; he presents a work in most graceful form and, in spite of the newly devised style, never strays too far from the middle point and always returns to it.[46]

The new manner also appears in Schubert's orchestration, which astonishes the critic because he imagines Schubert had heard few of his symphonies played (implying that the critic considers live performances the most reliable way to judge instrumentation):

It might be incomprehensible that Schubert had suddenly developed his effortless, brilliant mastery in dealing with the orchestra, if we did not know that this symphony was preceded by six others, and that he composed this one at the height of his mature powers [*in reifster Manneskraft*]. It must be attributed to his extraordinary talent, that he, who had heard so few of his instrumental works during his lifetime, attained such distinctive treatment of instruments amassed in the

[45] 'Die 7te Symphonie von Franz Schubert', *NZfM* xii (1840), 82.
[46] Ibid. 83.

orchestra, [instruments] which often speak contrastingly like human voices and chorus.[47]

The critic considers Schubert's approach to melodic–harmonic interweaving equally gifted and unusual. The C-major Symphony displays no concrete motivic links between movements in the Beethovenian sense; Schumann hears instead a general consistency of material which might be likened to that in a novel, 'one feels that the composer was the master of his story and that the coherence may well become clear to one in time'.[48]

Above all the novelty of the superficial idiom attracts Schumann. It prompts the critic to recall a 'tale' from his recent Viennese sojourn: he paints a fantastic picture of his visit to Schubert's grave and invokes memories of the Viennese hills, the cathedral and the Danube, all suffused with a Catholic incense wafting through the pages of the symphony. He continues, 'Here, apart from masterful musical technique in composition, lie all the various threads of life, colour in the finest gradations, overall significance, the most pointed expression of detail, and endless romanticism poured over the whole, such as [we] encounter elsewhere in Franz Schubert.'[49] Moreover, Schumann did not fail to note the reception accorded the new idiom by Leipzig's musical community, 'The symphony has affected us like no other since Beethoven's. Artists and friends of art were united in its praise . . .'.[50] This last comment suggests that Schumann has not really repudiated the basic Beethovenian foundations of the genre, no matter how much he stresses Schubert's autonomy. For the critic has no wish to question the inner consistency achieved by the symphonic web. Rather Schumann wishes recognition for a new orchestral speech, and he intimates, albeit distantly and indirectly, in a letter to Clara the possibility that the new idiom could form the basis for a stylistic tradition in which he might participate:

Clara, today I was blessed. A symphony by Franz Schubert was played today at rehearsal. If only you had been there. I cannot describe it to you; all the instruments are human voices, ingenious beyond measure, and this instrumentation quite independent of Beethoven— and the length, this heavenly length like a novel in four volumes, longer than the Ninth Symphony. I was quite happy, and wished for

[47] Ibid. 82–3.   [48] Ibid. 83.   [49] Ibid. 82.   [50] Ibid. 83.

nothing but that you might be my wife and that I could also write such symphonies.[51]

Schumann repeats the same sentiments to Ernest Becker, again implying the connection between success as a composer of a symphony inspired by Schubert's example and marriage, '[The Great C Major] has really pricked my ambition again to turn to the symphony soon, and if I am joyfully united with Clara, I think something will become of [this plan].'[52]

The relationship between Schumann's hopes of marrying Clara and the composition of a symphony requires some explanation. Schumann naturally attached great importance to the Gewandhaus as an artistic forum, and the symphony, as the most ambitious genre in that venue, would assume special prestige. In his case against Clara's marriage, Friedrich Wieck called Schumann's stature as a composer directly into question.[53] If Schumann could publish a substantial instrumental work, he would prove to Wieck, to his daughter, and to the public that the bitter charges were entirely mistaken.

Even this very selective account of the decade before the composition of Op. 38 shows that Schumann did not come to the Spring Symphony as an *ingénu*. His relatively successful experience with the G-minor Symphony provided him with practice in sketching orchestral music and in transferring his initial ideas to score. He taught himself orchestration both by reducing Beethoven and by establishing a method of empirical revision. He observed at first hand the potential for extraordinary performances of new orchestral literature at the Gewandhaus under the direction of Felix Mendelssohn, and he learned by participating in the arrangements for performing Schubert's Great C-major Symphony how such renditions could lead directly to publication. In his symphonic criticism he formulated his concept of a tradition with its basis in the Beethovenian web and in architectonic form, and he called for the development of new directions within the accepted framework. Through his office as editor Schumann searched consistently for the means of

[51] *Jugendbriefe*, pp. 307–8.
[52] Jansen, *Briefe*, p. 175.
[53] A concise account of the dispute between Robert and his father-in-law can be found in Peter Ostwald's *Schumann: The Inner Voices of a Musical Genius* (Boston, 1985), 151–6.

progress—a new orchestral style which would find acceptance with the public—discovering it finally in Schubert's work. During the decade before the composition of Op. 38, Schumann was involved, then, in an almost systematic process of experimentation and observation preparatory to composing. He required only a catalyst to fuse the elements of his preparation for symphonic writing into a finished piece, a catalyst supplied by events in his personal life.

2 The Process of Sketching and the Structure of the Spring Symphony

Although Schumann possessed a significant amount of experience in orchestral composition by the time of his marriage in the autumn of 1840, he had not actually engaged in sketching or scoring a symphony for almost seven years. His renewed hopes in this area led him to a number of exercises designed to recall his previous technical skills, and the first came in the form of 'symphonic attempts' recorded in his household accounts on 13 and 14 October 1840, just a month after his wedding.[1] Some writers assign a series of drafts now found in the Bonn University Library's miscellany *Schumann 19* to the autumn of 1840 (see the discussion of the fragment in C minor below), but it seems more likely that Schumann discarded his sketching from this period. In any event, the very mention of orchestral sketching in his household accounts gives evidence of his continuing interest in composing a symphony, an interest which also surfaces in the marital diary he kept with Clara:

9th week. 8–15 November 1840. The trip to Petersburg has been given up; we will go, perhaps, to Copenhagen. We speak much about Paris, and decided to go there later for a longer period. Let's leave it at that. Beforehand I would like to write a piano concerto and a symphony. I have enough songs (over one hundred)—can only tear myself away from them with difficulty. I have set the beautiful Rheinlied by Becker, the talk of all Germany; it appeared a few days ago.[2]

Mention of the 'Rheinlied' is significant only because Schumann orchestrated it on 27 November,[3] recultivating those skills in instrumentation left fallow for such a long time.

Just two months later Schumann began symphonic sketching

---

[1] *Haushaltbücher*, p. 164.

[2] Eugenie Schumann, *Robert Schumann: Ein Lebensbild meines Vaters* (Leipzig, 1931), 282.

[3] *Haushaltbücher*, p. 167. The piece appeared in 1840 without an opus number; see Alfred Dörffel, *Literarisches Verzeichnis der im Druck erschienenen Tonwerke von Robert Schumann*, supplement to *Musikalisches Wochenblatt*, i (1870), 36.

in earnest. His first attempt came on 21 January 1841, and the result can be seen in a torso of a first movement in C minor and three measures of a rondo in E-flat major, both found in the Bonn collection *Schumann 19*. Though Schumann later pencilled the date '(1840)' on the ink manuscript, this chronological assignment, coming after the fact, appears less convincing than his entry in the household accounts for 21 January about the 'beginning of a symphony in C minor' which describes the torso precisely. It seems highly unlikely that the entry could refer to the later C-minor Symphony of September 1841, as Gerd Nauhaus suggests.[4] Ex. 2.1*a* and *b* feature excerpts from the January torso, and I reproduce them in part to show that Schumann had not merely regained his technical facility in symphonic drafting, he now brought increasing sophistication to the task. The texture here, unlike that in Ex. 1.1 from the early 1830s, cannot be called pianistic, even though the page appears to be ruled for piano. Schumann follows the melodic thread rather than supplying a full reduction; the melodic line in the C-minor fragment connotes most of the harmonies to the composer, but when he wishes to remember a particular progression, he records the desired pitches briefly in the bass or enters sporadic triads, occasionally supplying a few measures of patterned figuration as a mnenomic aid. Notations about instrumental assignments suggest that the interplay of colour in the sketch forms a primary element in Schumann's conception of the piece.

Schumann abandoned this beginning for reasons we can never entirely know. Perhaps the slow introduction seemed too reminiscent of Haydn's 'London' Symphony[5] or the choice of key

---

[4] *Haushaltbücher*, p. 172; n. 210, p. 707. Nauhaus, transcriber and editor of the accounts, maintains that the entry refers to a fragment of scoring also included in *Schumann 19*. But Schumann clearly designates 23 September 1841 as the date of the sketch from which the score was orchestrated, and it is unlikely that the instrumentation occurred before the sketching. For details of this later piece, see my article, 'The Sketches for Robert Schumann's C Minor Symphony', *Journal of Musicology*, i (1982), 395–418.

[5] Several years later, when Schumann had found his own symphonic voice, he was not so obsesssed about avoiding the opening motive from Haydn's 'London' Symphony. He employs it, albeit disguised in an elaborate texture, as a part of the introduction to the Second Symphony, Op. 61. Whether he connected this fragment in C minor with the later introduction (also in C minor) to Op. 61 remains to be investigated, partly because we know so little about the sketching of the introduction. For an outline of the drafts for the first movement of Op. 61 see my article, 'The Sketches for the Fourth

Example 2.1*a* Schumann, excerpt from beginning of symphony fragment in C minor, Bonn, Schumann 19

and the initial theme appeared to appropriate the Beethovenian manner: in his criticism Schumann had expressly deplored the adoption of archaic (as opposed to progressive) symphonic styles.[6] None the less, he may not have counted all of the fragment as a loss, for two of the later themes bear passing resemblance to parts of Op. 38. The continuation of the torso in Ex. 2.1*b*, with its pronounced leap upward to a series of descending scales and its chromatic hemiola (albeit in ascending rather than descending motion) in measures 126 to 128, finds resonance in the second strain and the main theme of the scherzo proper from the First Symphony. These motivic similarities

Movement of Schumann's Second Symphony, Op. 61', *Journal of the American Musicological Society*, xxxix (1986), 149–52.

[6] He rejected at least one other symphonic draft in C minor later in 1841 because of its old-fashioned idiom; see my essay on 'Schumann's C Minor Symphony', p. 413.

Example 2.1*b*   Schumann, excerpt from continuation of symphony fragment in C minor, Bonn, Schumann 19

combined with a compositional technique like that used in the completed sketches for Op. 38 reinforce the notion that this C-minor fragment belongs in relatively close chronological proximity to the drafting of the Spring Symphony.

Schumann's imagination was primed, then, by the work on 21 January, and just two days after this initial attempt, the household accounts record the beginning of work on the First Symphony, completed in the frantic period of only four days. Given the intensity of the effort, the composer's first mention of the piece seems understated: he writes laconically on 23 January 1841, 'Spring Symphony begun'. The inner movements emerged together on the following day ('Adagio and Scherzo of the symphony finished'), a juxtaposition that led to many interrelationships between the pair. The finale took two days, according to the composer's ledgers which finally betray his growing excitement on 25 January, 'Symphonic fire— sleepless nights—on the last movement', and 26 January, 'Hurrah! Symphony finished!'.[7] Clara's entry in the common diary

---

[7] *Haushaltbücher*, pp. 172–3.

reinforces the impression left by the household accounts that Op. 38 resulted from a fit of inspiration, and Clara also provides the background for the symphony's programmatic title:

Today, Monday (25 January [*added in Robert's hand*]), Robert has almost finished his symphony; it appeared mostly during the night—my poor Robert had already spent a few sleepless nights on it. He calls it the 'Spring Symphony'—tender and poetic, as all of his musical thought is!—A poem about spring by * * [*sic*] gave the initial impetus for this creation. Tuesday, Robert finished his symphony; begun and completed, then, in four days. If only an orchestra were here! I must confess to you, my dear husband, that I would not have credited you with such facility—I respect you more and more!!!8

F. Gustav Jansen identifies the undisclosed poet in Clara's account as Adolf Böttger, a frequent guest in the Schumann household during this period and the librettist for *Das Paradies und die Peri*. His 'poem about spring' which inspired the composer runs:

Du Geist der Wolke, trüb' und schwer,
Fliegt drohend über Land und Meer,

Oh spirit of clouds, heavy and drear, that flies threateningly over land and sea,

Dein grauer Schleier deckt im Nu Des Himmels klares Auge zu,

Your grey veil hides at once Heaven's clear eye,

Dein Nebel wallt herauf von Fern Und Nacht verhüllt der Liebe Stern:

Your mists loom from afar And night envelops the star of love:

Du Geist der Wolke, trüb' und feucht, Was hast du all' mein Glück verscheucht,

Oh spirit of clouds, moist and drear, Why have you banished all my happiness,

Was rufft du Tränen in's Gesicht Und Schatten in der Seele Licht?

Why do you summon tears to my face And shadow to the light of my soul?

O wende, wende deinen Lauf,— Im Tale blüht der Frühling auf!

Oh turn, turn from your course,— In the valley spring bursts forth! 9

8 Berthold Litzmann, *Clara Schumann: Ein Künstlerleben nach Tagebüchern und Briefen*, 2nd edn. (Leipzig, 1903–8), 26–7.
9 F. Gustav Jansen, *Die Davidsbündler: aus Robert Schumann's Sturm- und Drangperiode* (Leipzig, 1883), 245.

An album leaf given to Böttger by Schumann bears an autograph of the introductory motto for trumpets and horns and the following inscription: 'Anfang einer Symphonie, durch ein Gedicht von Adolph Böttger veranlaßt. Dem Dichter zur Erinnerung von Robert Schumann. Leipzig in October 1842'. It may be that the rhythm for the opening fanfare of the first movement derives from the poetry.

Schumann also suggests a general programme for each movement of the symphony in the form of titles on the first page of the manuscript for Op. 38:

1. Frühlingsbeginn
2. Abend
3. Frohe Gespielen
4. Voller Frühling

Schumann usually declined to publish detailed programmes for his compositions, believing that written elucidations inhibited the full range of individual fantasy induced by absolute music. In Schumann's view such an indefinite and non-representational art found its very *raison d'être* in the freedom of imagination afforded the listener.[10] The composer did not reveal the evocative title for Op. 38 nor the mottos for the various movements to the concert-going public, though he mentioned the connection with spring to some contemporary acquaintances and performers. Even if the composer intended such mottos for limited consumption, however, they can provide useful information on the significance he attached to the piece. On the most superficial level, Schumann wrote the symphony during the winter in expectation of the coming season, according to his correspondence with Louis Spohr and Wilhelm Taubert.[11] But there is also a deeper, more personal symbolism connected with spring in Schumann's activity just prior to the sketching of the symphony. The composer was working jointly with Clara during January on a set of songs to texts from Friedrich Rückert's *Liebesfrühling*.[12] The image of spring represented the couple's

---

[10] See the composer's discussion of the programme for the *Symphonie fantastique* in the review, 'Aus dem Leben eines Künstlers' [etc.], pp. 49–51.

[11] See the letters to the two conductors in Erler, *Briefe*, i. 290–1, 293–4.

[12] The set appeared as Opus 37 in November 1841. See Dörffel, *Literarisches Verzeichnis*, p. 9.

new beginning in their recent marriage and a renewal of Robert's desire to become a major composer, an ambition frustratingly postponed by his quarrels with Wieck and work on the journal. The words 'Im Tale blüht der Frühling auf!' applied both to Schumann's private and professional life.

SKETCHES FOR THE FIRST MOVEMENT

The sketches from the productive period of late January 1841 can be found now in the Library of Congress under the catalogue number ML 96.S415 Case, together with the autograph of the initial scoring for Op. 38. After the composer's death Clara presented both sketches and score to the conductor Hermann Levi, whose family returned them to Schumann's heirs upon Levi's death in 1900.[13] In 1906 the combined manuscript became part of Wilhelm Heyer's collection, only to be sold at his death to the Library of Congress in 1926.[14] The sketches appear on unwatermarked paper in upright format 29.3 by 22.2 cm., and the leaves were heavily trimmed for the original binding, a process which partially or completely destroyed some of Schumann's marginalia.[15] The Library of Congress detached the leaves from the first binding, enclosing each in transparent library paper for the sake of preservation. As a result, we cannot ascertain the original foliation with complete confidence, but it appears that folio 7 is an extraneous leaf inserted after some sketching had been completed (this point will become clear later in the discussion of the Adagio). The manuscript presents continuity drafts for most of the symphony, as well as a very few short ideas for individual motives. A facsimile of the manuscript, both sketches and score, has been published by the Robert Owen Lehman Foundation,[16] and the foliation used here plainly appears

---

[13] Thus the inscription on the second folio of the manuscript, 'An Hermann Levi von/Clara Schumann.'

[14] See Georg Kinsky's description in *Versteigerung von Musiker-Autographen aus dem Nachlaß des Herrn Kommerzienrates Wilhelm Heyer in Köln . . . Montag, den 6. und Dienstag, den 7. Dezember 1926. . . durch Ernst Henrici & Leo Liepmannssohn. Antiquariat . . . Berlin*, 94.

[15] The best detailed description of the manuscript can be found in Georg Kinsky's *Musikhistorisches Museum von Wilhelm Heyer in Cöln* (Cologne, 1916), iv. 342–8.

[16] Robert Schumann, *Symphony, Opus 38* (New York, 1967).

in this photographic reproduction at the bottom left of each leaf.

In the sketches for the First Symphony, as in the aborted C-minor Symphony fragment, each system features paired staves with treble and bass clefs, and the texture on the initial page of drafting seems, at first glance, extremely full (see Illustration II). In fact, this texture did not result solely from the initial pass but from a series of revisions on this first page. Schumann began sketching in ink on what is now folio 4 of the manuscript, and he persisted in ink to number '16',[17] the end of the main theme (4^v, Illustration III). At this logical juncture Schumann apparently took pencil in hand and retouched the section he had just completed, changing the opening motive (a point to which we shall return momentarily) and otherwise suggesting some details about figuration in the slow introduction and main theme. He continued drafting the remainder of the symphony in pencil. Any notations in ink after measure '16' of the first movement were inserted when the composer orchestrated the score, and it also seems likely that some of the text in ink on the first page appeared during orchestration.[18]

A cursory glance at the sketch for the first movement reveals immediately that Schumann created a continuity draft almost without recourse to trial adumbrations or correction of the melodic thread. He proceeded directly because he had determined many of his compositional choices in advance. Drawing on the criteria he had formulated as a music critic, he selected his material from a current style, he worked this material by means of the motivic–harmonic weaving that constituted for him the essence of symphonic technique, and he articulated the results by means of an abstract architectonic framework.

To set the basic tone of the symphony Schumann selects from the very outset the new Schubertian manner so popular in Leipzig during 1839 and 1840: his introductory fanfare (Ex. 2.2) serves as an epigram invoking the Great C-major Symphony. Schubert's slow introduction opens with a dotted motto in the horns, first outlining a third above the tonic in scalar motion,

---

[17] I shall cite Schumann's own measure numbers in quotations throughout this discussion. The diagrams of structure for each movement also give approximate measure numbers for corresponding passages in the printed score.

[18] The composer added the second form of the opening motto in pencil and then inked over his pencilled entry during the process of instrumentation.

Example 2.2   Schumann, Op. 38, mvt. 1, sketch of opening fanfare

Example 2.3   Schubert, C-major Symphony, mvt. 1, opening horn melody

then the third below (Ex. 2.3), and after this opening *a due*, the harmonized and rescored melody repeats in the larger ensemble. Schumann adopts a similar dotted rhythmic conceit for the first version of his motto, which tests the third above the tonic and is repeated in the full orchestra. In his second pass through the draft he revises the sequence of pitches to create a version more cleverly and closely related to Schubert's, a varied reversal which outlines the third below the tonic in the horns and trumpets followed by an outline of the third above the tonic in the orchestral echo. Short of direct quotation, Schumann could not have been more obvious in this reference. He might just as well have written a programmatic paraphrase of his earlier statement to Clara at the head of the first movement, 'Now I shall write such a symphony!'

Two other features of the slow introduction specifically invoke Schubert's C-major Symphony. The first comes in reply to the opening motto: the answer consists essentially of a scale descending to a dramatically emphasized cadence on a D-minor chord (see Ex. 2.2). In this gesture Schumann invokes the mediant from the outset as a strong tonal focus, another feature he must have admired in Schubert's writing.[19] Schumann re-emphasizes this alternate tonal centre by modulating briefly to D major later in the introduction (4^r, sys. 5. m. 1), calling attention to the gesture with a flute cadenza on folio 4^r, system 4. The third and final segment of the sketched introduction (sys. 5–7, m. 2) moves from D major by common tone and chromatic alteration to an F major chord, the dominant of B flat, while accelerating in preparation for the main theme. This gradual transition over a figured string accompaniment represents yet another strong allusion to the beginning of the Great C-major Symphony; Schumann had specifically admired the effect in his 1840 review.[20]

If Schumann employs dotted motives, harmonic colour, and gesture in the introduction to establish the Schubertian manner, the manipulation of this material to form the exposition stems from a tradition the composer regards as Beethovenian. Schumann's creation of the symphonic web finds its most obvious expression in the main theme (see Ex. 2.4). Its head motive clearly derives from the opening fanfare, and its companion reply from the introduction, a descending scale, appears here disguised by ornamentation in the treble part. Schumann displays this pattern twice as perfectly symmetrical and identical eight-measure phrases: the antecedent moves from tonic to dominant (mm. '1–8'), and the consequent, a simple transposition of the first unit, moves from subdominant back to the tonic (mm. '9–16'). To overcome the self-contained nature of these interlocking phrases, Schumann carries his reference into the ensuing transition. Again, the motto from the opening fanfare is readily apparent (mm. '16–17'), while the composer has disguised the answering scale, this time by means of inversion (mm. '18–20'). The last example of motivic cleverness provides more than coherence between various segments of the movement; it displays the inventiveness and quick wit that determine the exuberant mood of the Spring Symphony.

Where Schumann does not appropriate material from the introduction to create the symphonic web, he develops the implications of the introduction's harmonic patterns, as he does

[19] The harmonic scheme of Schubert's exposition for the first movement of the Great C-major Symphony, for instance, includes a prominent progression from the first theme in C major to a secondary theme in E minor (mm. 134–50) before proceeding to the closing in G.

[20] 'Die 7te Symphonie von Franz Schubert', *NZfM*, xii (1840), 83.

Example 2.4   Schumann, Op. 38, mvt. 1, sketch of main theme

in the secondary theme. We can easily detect such tonal developments in the sketch by the presence of harmonic bass lines (as opposed to those of melodic significance). By the end of the first transition (see Table 2 for a structural outline of the first movement) Schumann arrives in his draft on a C pedal (dominant of F major) by means of a particularly forceful motion: the preparation consists of an augmented-sixth chord based on the D flat denoted faintly in the bass at measure '61' on 4^{v}.[21] Instead of moving directly to the key implied by the

[21] To outline the harmonic motion of the transition more precisely, the composer moves from a dominant seventh chord on F by means of common tones (C, E flat) to

TABLE 2. *Outline of the sketch for the first movement of Op. 38*

Section	Theme	Key	Location (fo. sys.)	Schumann's Nos.	Score mm.
Exposition	Introduction	I–III–I	4^r, 1–7	—	1–38
	Main theme	I	4^r, 7–4^v, 1	1–16	39–54
	Transition 1	x	4^v, 1–5	17–24, 56–72	55–80
	Secondary theme	(vii)–V	4^v, 5–7	73–88	81–95
	Transition 2	x	4^v, 7–5^r, 2	88–108	96–117
	Closing theme	V	5^r, 2–5	109–116	118–133
Development & Recapitulation	Model 1	x	5^r, 5–6	25–32	134–141
	sequence		5^r, 6–8	33–40	142–149
	Model 2		5^r, 8–5^v, 1	41–48	150–157
	sequence		5^v, 1–2	49–55	158–165
	Bridge 1		5^v, 2–3	—	166–177
	Main theme	III	5^v, 3–6	1–[24]	178–201
	Models & sequences 1–2	x	5^v, 6–6^r, 2	25–55	202–232
	Bridge 2	x	6^r, 2–4	—	233–293
	Retransition	x–I	6^r, 4–6	—	294–316
	Transition 1	x	6^r, 6–8	[17–72]	317–343
	Secondary theme	(iii)–I	6^r, 8–6^v, 1	[73–88]	344–358
	Transition 2	x	6^v, 2–4	[88–108]	359–380
	Closing theme	I	6^v, 4–5	[109]–116	—
Coda		I	7^r	—	381–515

horn calls, the composer casts the first phrase of the secondary theme in A minor hinting strongly of D minor[22] (see Ex. 2.5), and even though he arrives clearly in F major at measure '80', he ends the section with a deceptive cadence on a D-minor chord in measure '88'[23] Schumann explicitly notes all these

---

an A-flat triad. This chord acts as a the dominant of D flat, and this pitch in turn becomes the root of the augmented-sixth chord.

[22] The parallel passage in the recapitulation actually appears briefly in D minor by virtue of the transposition discussed later, see p. 44.

[23] The sketch clearly shows a syncopated D-minor chord at this juncture, but Schumann gives a B-flat-major chord on the downbeat of his score by placing root in the lone second oboe (m. 96). The momentary clash between the B flat in the oboe and the A in the violas again displays the dichotomy between the two harmonies. A deceptive cadence results in either case, preserving momentum into the ensuing transition with its new arpeggiated motive, harmonic and thematic instability.

Example 2.5   Schumann, Op. 38, mvt. 1, sketch of second theme

harmonic idiosyncracies in the draft of the secondary theme, producing the peculiarly full texture of this passage. The hint of D minor is a deliberate reference to the introduction's tonal progression from the tonic B flat, to the dominant F, by way of the mediant D. Both on melodic and harmonic levels Schumann follows the implications of his opening gesture with a kind of relentless musical logic that constitutes the very essence of the symphonic tradition according to his writings.

The composer continues the traditional interweaving in his closing theme for the exposition (mm. '109–16', Illustration IV) with the dotted figure and scalar motion which originate in the reply to the opening fanfare, displaying yet again the distant kinship with the pervasive dotted rhythms in the first movement of the Great C-major Symphony. Schumann's only moment of hesitation here comes in deciding the proportion of the closing cadences. The continuity draft displays a rather abrupt ending for the section on folio 5^r, system 4, measure 3. Schumann apparently feels the need of more repetition to balance the weight of the exposition: after fashioning a first ending that initially features a quotation from the rhythm of the opening fanfare, he appends a series of repeated caesura chords and then carries the idea into the second ending on the next system. This small doubt about proportion seems insignifcant when compared with the composer's confidence in the synthesis of the style and technique which allowed him to produce the rest of the exposition so decisively.

Schumann's highly abstract notion of architectonic form aids him in proceeding through the remainder of the movement with the same dispatch and assurance that mark the exposition. The composer begins the development by creating a long modulating unit. His first model derives from the main theme and serves as a bridge (see Ex. 2.6); two statements of the initial motto beginning on B flat (mm. '25–8') are followed by four measures of a prolonged diminished chord, over which the second measure of the motto repeats three times (mm. '29–31'). This configuration then repeats in sequence, and the composer moves to a new eight-measure model featuring a fragment from the beginning of the motto, this time with a countermelody on D (mm. '41–8'). Moving around the circle of fifths, the sequence (mm. '49–55') begins on G and heads toward C. The ensuing two-measure fragmentation (5ᵛ, systems 2–3, Illustration V) rises sequentially by step from C to the E which becomes the fifth in an A-major chord serving as dominant to D major (see Table 2). The modulating unit is remarkable for the temporal regularity of its models and sequences, and for the calculated tonal progress from B flat at the beginning to the D which predominates towards the end; the motion rehearses yet again the harmonic crux of the movement.

After the creation of the basic developmental unit, Schumann begins the process of repeating material according to an abstract plan that we can reconstruct by following the logic of the numerals he inserted in the sketch. He first decides on a deceptive gesture that makes a tonal point: citation of the main theme in the key of D major (as well as a small portion of the first transition). To facilitate this repetition the composer returns to the exposition and labels measures '1' to '24' with arabic numerals. He then goes back to the sketch of the development and enters an incipit for the main theme in the key of 'D' on the verso of folio 5, together with some notes about new figuration in the violins, the arabic numerals '1' and '2', and

Example 2.6   Schumann, Op. 38, mvt. 1, sketch of initial developmental segment

barlines for 24 measures. After this recapitulation in the major mediant, Schumann repeats the initial developmental unit, almost as if he were beginning the whole section again.[24] He labels the first 31 measures of the development, beginning where he had left off earlier, with arabic '25' and continuing to '55'. He then inserts a '25' on the verso of folio 5 (Illustration V), indicates F natural as the starting point of the first model, and leaves 31 blank measures. The end of this literal reprise leaves him at the pitch level of G, requiring a bridge to the retransition with material drawn from the closing area of the exposition.

[24] Anthony Newcomb discusses the disorientation occasioned by this kind of displacement in 'Schumann and Late Eighteenth-Century Narrative Strategies', *19th Century Music*, xi (1987), 164–74.

The retransition takes shape in the opening fanfare and prepares one of the most delicious instances of the wit found throughout the First Symphony. Schumann indicates a citation of the slow introduction by inserting a double bar on folio 6ʳ (see Illustration VI) to prepare a return of common time and slower tempo ('Un poco . . . Adagio [*in the far right margin*]'). As in its first appearance, the fanfare acts here as herald of the main theme. But even before the trumpets have sounded, the main theme has stolen on to the scene in the midst of the development, and for this reason Schumann moves directly from the retransition to an incipit for measure '17' of the exposition after the dramatic D-minor cadence on (6ʳ, sys. 6).[25] Here the composer notes a transposition ('Quart höher'[fourth higher]) and a repeat of the remainder of the exposition almost to the end of the closing section. He has already used the arabic numerals '25' to '55' for labelling part of the development to this point, and therefore he tags the remainder of his exposition beginning with '56'. Following the numeral '116' at the end of the recapitulation, Schumann inserts a tonic seventh chord in first inversion, indicating that the material on 6ᵛ Illustration VII) does not conclude the sketch. But he produces no continuity draft for the coda: an extraneous sheet of paper later included in this manuscript as folio 7 merely preserves his few brief ideas for the first movement's close (see Ex. 2.7).[26]

Schumann's system of labelling structural repetition displays his concept of architectonic form with striking clarity. He consciously chooses D as a false key for the recapitulation of the main theme, working from the tonal logic of his slow introduction with its mediant tonal emphasis. (The gesture also alludes to the tonally deceptive recapitulation in the last movement of

[25] In a recent article about Schumann's sketches, Akio Mayeda makes much of the 'thematic ambiguity' of this passage which he views as both opening fanfare and recapitulation of the main theme. In his draft Schumann unambiguously indicates a citation of the fanfare by his change of time signature and resulting double bars. In the scored version he sets the beginning of the section over a dominant pedal, a classic sign of retransition, not recapitulation; if we miss the signal, we miss the delightful sport. For Mayeda's discussion of this passage and some others in the first movement, see 'Die Skizzen Robert Schumanns als stilkritische Erkenntnisquelle', *Robert Schumann—Ein romantisches Erbe in neuer Forschung* (Mainz, London, New York, Tokyo, 1984), 119–39.

[26] I recount my reasons below for supposing that this page did not form part of the initial draft of the manuscript; see the discussion of Schumann's revised last measure in the Adagio, p. 50–1.

Example 2.7   Schumann, Op. 38, mvt. 1, sketch of idea for coda

Schubert's C-major Symphony, m. 598.) He arranges the return to the tonic after the retransition using the same technique, simply transposing a whole unit beginning on a pitch level which will automatically lead back to a conclusion on the tonic. The manipulation of sketched musical material in blocks, as if different components of a building had been rearranged in a blueprint, reveals the precision of Schumann's structural calculations and also recalls Schumann's concept of form in his article on the first movement of Berlioz's *Symphonie fantastique.* There he sees Berlioz's formal arch as a repositioning of elements from a more traditional blueprint, and something of this abstract symmetry can be seen in Schumann's own draft. He calls attention to his unusual choice of key for the recapitulation of the main theme by surrounding it with two identical musical units (sets of developmental bridges), at the same time engendering a pointed interplay between the conventional formal scheme and the unfolding events.

Schumann's heavy reliance on highly abstract architectonic concepts would not be so extraordinary in the draft were it not coupled with his fondness for certain features of Schubertian rhetoric. Schubert shows a predilection in the Great C-major Symphony—as he does in many other instrumental pieces—for sudden reversals, disruptions, and themes delimited by strongly invoked closure (particularly good examples of these features can be found at joins in the first movement, mm. 131–4, and the last movement, mm. 160–4). These disjunctions do not interrupt the flow of Schubert's composition severely, for his technique of constructing themes from relatively slow melodic lines moving over repetitious accompanimental patterns tends to build an inertia that implies continuity. The sudden reversals and pronounced caesuras at the conclusions of such units come almost as a relief rather than a disturbance. But Schumann's very brief themes, with their witty harmonic feints and short, interlocking phrases, appear pointedly disconnected in an atmosphere combining dramatic Schubertian pauses with architectonic abstraction. While we might view disjunction as a fault in the sketches of the first movement, it lies, ironically, at the heart of Schumann's inspiration for the symphony. Schumann seems to have considered Schubert's abrupt rhetoric and fresh orchestral idiom appropriate to the subject of spring. If Schumann had masked his architectonic form in seamless transitions, the first movement would lose much of its vitality. The somewhat mechanical nature of the form is bound inextricably to the music's wit, charm, and to the effectiveness of its formal interplay. We can easily understand the composer's decision at the end of this sketch on 23 January to draft the rest of the symphony, using this first movement as a secure point of departure.

SKETCHES FOR THE SECOND AND THIRD MOVEMENTS

Schumann's penchant for the thematic interconnection of disparate symphonic segments in Op. 38 is exemplified most clearly by the sketches for the inner movements conceived together on 24 January; they form an interlude of common motivic content and rhythmic gesture separating the outer pair. Schumann begins by labelling the second movement 'Idylle' in his sketches (see Illustration VIII), reinforcing its function as a foil to the first movement. He casts this slow movement in the sub-dominant key of E-flat major, and alludes to his programmatic title by using 6/8 meter with its pastoral connotations. At some point he changes his original tempo marking of 'Andante' to 'Larghetto' and correspondingly doubles the note values by writing 'Nach 6/4tel' at the head of the sketch after he finishes his first pass, for he notates the whole draft in 6/8 time. Schumann elides two conventions for slow movements, the theme and variation and ternary form, to produce a structure in which a main theme appears three times over an increasingly ornamented accompaniment, with the middle variation in the dominant key (see Table 3).

TABLE 3. *Outline of the sketch for the second movement of Op. 38*

Section	Key	Location (fo., sys.)	Schumann's Nos.	Score mm.
Main theme	I	8ʳ, 1–3, m.3	1–7	1–23
Transition	x	8ʳ, 3–4, m.5	—	23–40
Variation 1	V	8ʳ, 5–6, m.2	—	41–55
Transition	x	8ʳ, 6–8, m.5	—	55–77
Variation 2	I	8ʳ, right margin	1–7	78–100
Coda (first version)	I	8ᵛ, 1–2	—	—
(revised version)	I	3ᵛ, 1	—	100–113
(bridge)	x	8ᵛ, 3	—	113–123

For his main theme Schumann chooses a phrase structure typical of symphonic slow movements, a period.[27] In the sketch he indicates both the melody and the sinuous contrapuntal bass, adding figures occasionally as a reminder about harmony (see Ex. 2.8). The proportions are conventional: a four-measure antecedent phrase rises to a cadence on the dominant, and a consequent four-measure phrase replies by falling back to the point of origin. Consequent phrases commonly repeat the head motive of the antecedent in such periodic structures, and Schumann follows this basic procedure by introducing an indicative variation: the beginning of the consequent phrase is an ornamented and largely inverted play on the beginning of the antecedent. The relationship between the beginning of the first two phrases is consistent with Schumann's general melodic grammar which often makes use of motivic inversion and depends on constant change of direction for much of its interest. Normally, the consequent phrase would cadence on the tonic, but Schumann chooses a deceptive close for measure 8 in order to repeat the last four measures, adjusted this time to create an authentic close. The composer gives the first variation to the cellos, taking advantage of the transposition to form the dominant key which places the melodic line comfortably in the baritone range. He uses only the first seven measures of the main theme

---

[27] For a discussion of phrase structure commonly used by German composers during the late eighteenth and early nineteenth centuries see Erwin Ratz, *Einführung in die musikalische Formenlehre: Über Formprinzipien in den Inventionen und Fugen J.S. Bachs und ihre Bedeutung für die Kompositionstechnik Beethovens*, 3rd edn. (Vienna, 1973), 24 ff.

Example 2.8   Schumann, Op. 38, mvt. 2, sketch of main theme

*Brackets indicate entry in ink during orchestration.

here, omitting the repetition of the consequent phrase, a precedent he then follows for the final variation indicated by the numbers '1–7' at the bottom of 8r.[28] Again in this system of labelling measures we see Schumann's strong reliance on concepts of architectonic form.

The most striking features of the second movement are the rhythmic and harmonic content of its theme. The draft plainly shows the hemiola that constitutes the central rhythmic conceit of the movement. One of Schumann's favourite metrical devices in his large-scale instrumental works,[29] it manifests itself most graphically in these sketches because of the compound time signature. The composer accentuates the hemiola by reiterating the figure in sequence during the course of the antecedent phrase. The main theme also contains a notable harmonic gesture, a recurrently stressed D flat (the lowered seventh degree) used

[28] In the scored version, however, he restores the repetition.
[29] His Piano Concerto, Op. 54 and the E-flat-major Symphony, Op. 97 offer just two prominent examples.

either as the minor seventh of a passing tonic chord in third inversion (m. '2') or as the fifth of a diminished chord built on G (m. '4') resolving to a sub-dominant chord in first inversion. These colourful progressions suggest a reason (apart from contrapuntal considerations) why the composer sketches the bass in such detail for the initial period. The D flat, often followed directly by the D natural of the dominant, lends this movement its special poignancy and, in combination with the hemiola rhythm, its sense of quiet unrest.

To move between the main theme and its variations, Schumann constructs two relatively lengthy transitions. These sketches of the transitions record his initial plans to use an accelerating accompanimental figuration to impart a sense of forward motion. The appearance of sixteenth notes beginning on the third system of 8^r and the thirty-second notes on the sixth and seventh systems signal the adoption of this increasingly active decoration. (The composer added the note about '32stele' for the violas at the beginning of the draft much later in ink as he transferred the theme to the score. As we shall see, he ultimately regretted this alteration and returned to the logic of his original conception.)[30] Schumann apparently required only this brief reminder of the plan; he leaves most of the detailed work to the process of orchestration. The sketch of the first transition also yields a significant piece of material in the form of a motive (Ex.2.9a), later transformed (Ex. 2.9b) in the transition from variation 1 to variation 2. The first version of the motive contains two quarter notes falling a fourth with two eighth notes rising a third. In its transformed state the falling fourth has been preserved but the eighth notes now descend by steps. Transformed yet again

Example 2.9a   Schumann, Op. 38, mvt. 2, sketch of motive from first transition

[recte: G]

Example 2.9*b*   Schumann, Op. 38, mvt. 2, sketch of transformed motive in second transition

(Ex. 2.10, mm. 3–6), this motive serves the composer as the material for a bridge from the second to the third movement and, subsequently, as a subject for the main theme of the third movement.

The process of conjoining the two inner movements in the draft most prominently displays Schumann's conscious creation of a motivic web. The precise sequence in the construction of the coda to the second movement and transition to the third movement cannot be determined with absolute certainty, but I will venture a series of steps that seems most likely based on the position of entries in the manuscript. At first Schumann imagines a conventional codetta (top of 8ᵛ; see Illustration IX) containing a final melodic flourish and cadence (Ex. 2.10). But after he completes this ending, he hits upon the notion of linking the second movement with the third by means of a bridge, and he fashions a passage for trombones and woodwinds (Ex. 2.10, sys. 2) which connects to the *penultimate* measure of the codetta, borrowing its material from the second transition in the 'Larghetto'. Schumann alters the motive taken from the second movement's transition for the bridge (the dotted B flat and ensuing E-flat anticipation) by ascending a fourth from an anacrusis rather than descending a fourth from the first beat (compare Exx. 2.10 and 2.9*b*); the descending scale from the transition motive appears in a chromatic version. Schumann next composes the opening of the third movement, using the material from the bridge for the head motive of the main theme. But at some point, perhaps after the completion of the Scherzo or even the whole sketch, he decides to alter the ending of the second movement. He deletes the last two measures of his 'I Var.[iation]' and composes a new version of these measures with much calmer

Example 2.10   Schumann, Op. 38, mvt. 2, sketch of first version of coda and bridge to mvt. 3

melodic motion (Ex. 2.11), entering his alternative on the nearest piece of unused paper available in the manuscript, the back of the title page (see Table 3).[31] This revised version of the ending to the second movement leads much more gradually to the bridge, gives a much clearer melodic outline, and gradually introduces the chromatic movement which will play an essential part in the measures to follow. At the same time, the sustained dominant seventh chord inhibits a sense of complete repose at the end of the second movement, impelling us gently into the bridge.

The sketches show Schumann's extraordinary compositional dexterity here in transforming the sentimental tones of the 'Idylle' into the aggressive harmonic and rhythmic wit of the

[31] The location of the insertion on the back of the title page leads to the sequence suggested above. Schumann must have sketched the trombone bridge, the Scherzo, and at least the beginning of the trio before entering this passage on the back of the title page, or he would have written his insertion on 8ᵛ underneath the old coda. His placement of the revised passage on the back of the title page suggests that folio 7 was not originally part of the manuscript draft, for had this leaf been present when Schumann composed the alternate version, he would have entered his insertion on the nearest blank page, i.e. 7ᵛ. Instead, he used the back of the title page. One other bit of evidence reinforces this conclusion: while 7ᵛ obviously blotted a large amount of ink from some proximate leaf at one time, the facing page of sketches, 8ʳ, was written in pencil. Folio 7 was probably a free piece of scrap paper lying unattached in Schumann's studio while he worked on Op. 38. We cannot draw any firm conclusions about the chronology of the material appearing on it from its present placement in the manuscript.

Example 2.11   Schumann, Op. 38, mvt. 2, sketch of second version of coda on 3ᵛ

third movement. His modulation over the course of the bridge (Ex. 2.10, sys. 2) ends with repeated plagal cadences in D major, and this device, sufficiently reiterated, calls the tonic into question by presenting the sub-dominant as a false tonic. Schumann continues this conceit in the Scherzo by placing its tonic chord, D minor, on an upbeat and landing heavily on the first downbeat with a G-minor chord (Ex. 2.12). G minor seems at first hearing to be the tonic, a matter which the half-cadence on A in measure 8 does little to clarify; the composer does not supply a clear arrival until the authentic cadence on D at the end of the first strain.

Schumann enhances the poignancy of this tonal deception by vehement employment of the hemiola introduced at the beginning of the second movement and featured in the bridge. The interplay of accentuation can be seen easily in Schumann's draft: the bass notes in the first four measures of the theme fall on the downbeat of each two-measure grouping, emphasizing the

Example 2.12   Schumann, Op. 38, mvt. 3, sketch of first phrase, main theme of scherzo proper

pitches in a G-minor triad. Schumann clouds the progression to A in measures 5 through 7 by taking up his hemiola pattern in the bass, offset one beat. In his second layer of sketching he makes the melody conform to the rhythmically deceptive bass. By displacing the rhythm in this way, Schumann transforms the placid hemiola of the second movement into a more forceful statement in the third movement. The chromatic melody in D minor, adopted from the bridge, adds to the tension of the rhythmic interplay: in reserving the half-step descent until the very end of each two-measure unit, Schumann enhances the sense of propulsion in the first strain. The combined techniques engender the most forward striving of all German phrase structures, the *Satz*.[32] To achieve the more balanced and contained phrasing typical of main themes in scherzos, Schumann repeats this first eight-measure unit at the octave in his sketches, but leads the cadence to the tonic this time. The two sentences together form a stable period containing equal antecedent and consequent phrases comprising a closed first strain (see Table 4).

The second strain of the Scherzo adopts a head-motive similar to that of the first strain, but by way of generating contrast Schumann displays the idea in a diatonic form without the rhythmic complications of hemiola. The composer finally extends the downward motion by means of a gentle scale before rounding the second strain (the repetition is indicated at the end of system

TABLE 4. *Outline of the sketch for the third movement of Op. 38*

Section	Strain	Phrase	Key	Location (fo., sys.)	Score mm.
Scherzo:	1	a–a'	i	8^v, 4–5, m. 8	1–16
	2	b–a–a'	III–i	8^v, 5–7	17–48
Trio	1	c	I	8^v 8–9^r, 1, m. 6	49–63–79*
	2	d	x–^{b}III–I	9^r, 1–7	80–155–231*
Coda		b'–c	I	9^r, 8–9^v, 4	361–408

* In most modern scores the repetition of each strain is written out, as is the Scherzo da capo.

32 See Ratz, *Einführung*, pp. 24 ff.

7 on 8^v by the brief instruction 'bis' and a '*fine*' sign keyed to the last measure of the first strain, see Table 4). The juxtaposition of the descending scale at the beginning of the second strain with the hemiola and chromaticism that rounds the segment may seem familiar because the same general ideas appear together in Ex. 2.1*b* from the C-minor Symphony, possibly sketched on 21 January just a few days before this movement. Taken as a whole, the cleverness and economy of this Scherzo most resemble Schumann's earlier music for piano, much of which alluded to the dance (especially *Papillons, Carnaval*, and the *Davidsbündlertänze*). The phrases display highly regular external proportions and cadence clearly and correctly. The eccentricity so charming in Schumann's music—strong rhythmic juxtapositions, tonal misdirection, and subtle melodic development—resides within the confines of these regular phrases.

If the scherzo proper presents a witty development of the material in the second movement, the trio carries the principle of interconnection beyond the confines of the internal movements by referring to the harmonic and thematic content of the first movement. At the same time, the trio accords us one of the more revealing glimpses of Schumann's compositional technique. The composer creates a distinctive morph (or composite shape) for this movement consisting of a D-major chord reiterated as a quarter-note anacrusis followed by a half and a concluding quarter (see Ex. 2.13). The melody of this cell alludes to the first three notes of the opening fanfare from the first movement, preserving its initial anacrusis, extended second note, and ensuing shorter note, that is to say, the dotted rhythm plus its pick-up all on a single pitch. The choice of D major for the chord recalls the first movement's prominent display of the key and suggests in retrospect that the D minor of the scherzo proper also refers to the opening allegro (an allusion merely obscured at first hearing by harmonic misdirection). Taken as a pair, the scherzo and trio feature the interplay between D minor and major that permeates the first movement.

Because Schumann builds the whole trio from a chordal morph and its variants, he records it just briefly at the beginning of the draft. Much of the remaining adumbration refers to the manipulation of the motive at various pitch levels by recording the changing root of the triad in the bass. The sketch also

Example 2.13 Schumann, Op. 38, mvt. 3, sketch of trio beginning

gives the proportions of phrases (sometimes exactly, sometimes approximately) in the form of blank measures and repeat signs (see Illustration X). Schumann makes further notations about the actual material content only where he wishes a bit of contrapuntal working or some minor variation in the shape of the basic motto (systems 4, 6, and 7). At first glance we may believe that Schumann leaves much to chance in this passage, but in fact he simply avoids useless scrivening. The manuscript served its creator as a series of shorthand reminders, and for this reason we cannot take it all literally. In reading it we must interpret it as its author did when he used it to compose a scored version.[33]

While Schumann indicates the traditional repeat of the scherzo proper with the usual laconic 'da capo' (9ʳ, sys. 7), he must write out the draft of his coda for the third movement because it features new combinations of material from both the scherzo

---

[33] This point relates generally to the manner in which these sketches must be transcribed: they cannot be rendered diplomatically if we wish to make sense of their content. I have referred to this problem in the preface and again cite Gossett's discussion in 'Beethoven's Sixth Symphony: Sketches for the First Movement', *Journal of the American Musicological Society*, xxvii (1974), 280.

proper and the trio. The quotations appear in interrupted alternation, as if Schumann could not choose an ending, a conceit which absorbs the inertia of the relentless scherzo proper and serves to close the third movement quietly. The composer's feigned indecision begins at the bottom of folio 9ʳ with a citation from the second strain of the scherzo proper, and continues on the verso with an ornamented bit of the trio, 'Un poco piu Adagio' (see Illustration XI). A simple cadential passage ('Andante', sys. 2–3) ends in a final ironic allusion to the chordal trio, itself a veiled reference to the motto from the first movement. Schumann casts the coda, like the trio, in D major, and his closing quip places this harmony in its most poignant juxtaposition to the B-flat major resumed in the last movement.

Sketches for the Fourth Movement

For his finale Schumann sketches a counterpart to the first movement invoking the variety of metaphoric relationship between the outer pair that had provided, in his view, coherence between the movements of Schubert's Great C-major Symphony.[34] Schumann maintains the symphonic web here not by means of explicit harmonic or melodic citation, but rather by employing similar gesture, rhetoric, and tone. He establishes the relationship from the very outset with a spectacular gesture like the one at the beginning of the first movement, in this case an introductory flourish rather than a brass fanfare. The sketches suggest that the effect occurred to Schumann independently, before he began the continuity draft of the last movement. His initial idea for the flourish appears on the verso of folio 7 (see Ex. 2.14), the same piece of scrap paper on which the composer had recorded the ideas for the coda in the first movement (see Table 2). Just as Schumann had used the fanfare in the first movement as the source of material for the exposition, he draws musical ideas for later portions of the fourth movement from its opening flourish. The two main ideas include the opening arpeggio and an ascending scale featuring a prominent syncopation (see Ex. 2.15 and Illustration XI). In the draft a flute cadenza follows the flourish (9ᵛ, sys. 5, m. 5–6), another gesture

---

[34] See the discussion of his review of Schubert above, p. 26.

Example 2.14   Schumann, Op. 38, mvt. 4, sketch of initial idea for flourish on 7^v

Example 2.15   Schumann, Op. 38, mvt. 4, sketch of opening flourish and excerpt from main theme

reminiscent of the introduction to the first movement (see 4^r, sys. 4). Schumann may use the solo flute in these two situations as a mild reference to the sounds of birds in spring, but this second cadenza has consequences beyond aural allusion, for the highly figured main theme of the fourth movement grows out of the flute's passage work. In this sense, we can regard the main theme of the fourth movement as resulting in a subtle way from the implications of melodic ideas found in the first.

The sketch of the main theme shows one of Schumann's few hesitations over phrase structure in this movement. After completing fifteen measures of the theme, the composer imagines a conventional repeat of the phrase beginning with the three eighth notes leading to the fourth measure on the recto of folio 10 (see Illustration XII). But he immediately abandons this notion in favour of spinning out his figuration at irregular length, adding a codetta at the end (mm. '25–31') with the usual repeated cadential figures. The disjunction here, created by a rest in all parts, reminds us again of the pauses between major sections in Schubert's C-major Symphony, and Schumann's sketch further emphasizes his conception of strong division with the presence of a double bar separating the main theme from the transition. Where the main theme of the first movement tends to be self-contained by virtue of its interlocking, perfectly symmetrical phrases, the first theme in the finale achieves the same separation by means of the rhetorical pause at its conclusion. They share the strong closure produced by accented authentic cadences reinforced by change of instrumentation.

Schumann again relies on the symphonic web to promote continuity and coherence in his transition and second theme. For the transition he combines a rhythmic motive from the close of the main theme with a portion of the opening flourish in minor mode (Ex. 2.16), and later appropriates the opening motive from the main theme, all in order to bridge the gap created by the grand pause. He connects the second theme to the transition by superimposing the syncopated rhythms from the flourish on the second theme's head motive (Ex. 2.17), and he uses the flourish's opening as both a cadential figure at the end of the first phrase and also as an anacrusis to the second. The composer ends his sketch for this brief exposition with a repeated set of arpeggiated closing figures (10^v, sys. 5; see Illustration XIII). He appends a

Example 2.16   Schumann, Op. 38, mvt. 4, sketch of excerpt from transition

Example 2.17   Schumann, Op. 38, mvt. 4, sketch of excerpt from second theme

short retransition to the exposition, then deletes it and reproduces instead a version of the earlier flute cadenza for the violins on the sixth system of folio 10ᵛ. (He calls attention to this revision by writing 'NB. 4 Tacte' and noting 'violno'.) While the exposition resembles that of the first movement in its rhetoric and musical gesture, it is smaller in proportion (see Table 5) and less involved in harmonic working. Schumann concentrates in the finale on tonic-subdominant-dominant relationships between major themes, as if the conventional interconnections were more appropriate for the conclusion of the whole symphony.

TABLE 5. *Outline of the sketch for the fourth movement of Op. 38*

Section	Theme	Key	Location (fo., sys.)	Schumann's Nos.	Score. mm.
Introduction:	Flourish	I	9ᵛ, 5–6.	—	1–6
Exposition:	Main theme	I	9ᵛ, 6–10ʳ, 5	1–31	7–42
	Transition	x	10ʳ, 5–10ᵛ, 1.	32–53	43–65
	Secondary theme	V	10ᵛ, 1–4	54–76	66–89
	Closing theme	V	10ᵛ, 5	77–81	89–96
	First ending	x	10ᵛ, 6	—	97–100
	Second ending	x	10ᵛ, 7, mm. 1–4	—	97–100
Development:	Bridge	x	10ᵛ, 7–11ʳ, 1, m. 3	—	101–116
	Model 1		11ʳ, 1–3	1–16	117–132
	Sequence 1		11ʳ, 3–5, m. 4	1–[16]	133–148
	frag. (6 × 2)		11ʳ, 5–6	—	149–169
	Retransition & Cadenza		11ʳ, 7–11ᵛ,	—	170–177
Recapitulation:	Main theme	I	11ᵛ, 2–7	1–31	178–213
	Transition	x	11ᵛ, 7–12ʳ, 1	32–[53]	214–237
	Secondary theme	I	12ʳ, 1–4	[54–76]	238–261
	Closing theme	I	12ʳ, 5–6	[77]–81	261–268
Coda:	Model 2	I–x	12ʳ, 5–8	82–89	269–296
	Sequence 2	x	12ᶜ, 1–4	82–89	297–316
	Cadences	I	12ᵛ, 4–8	—	317–347

With the exposition complete, Schumann's mechanical technique of deploying his material reasserts itself. After the second ending (10ᵛ, sys. 7. mm. 1–4), he drafts a fourteen-measure bridge which features some motivic recombination of its own and also serves to establish the beginning pitch of D flat for the development's core. The composer delineates the central model-sequence grouping in his sketch with a double barline at the top of folio 11, where he creates a sixteen-measure unit from a series of shorter sequences (see Ex. 2.18 and Illustration XIV). He begins with four measures of material derived from the opening flourish worked contrapuntally, and he repeats this segment a whole tone up (mm. '5–8'; the E-flat initiation appears in octave transposition). For the remaining eight measures of this core he uses material more akin to the second theme, woven

Example 2.18 Schumann, Op. 38, mvt. 4, sketch of developmental model and implied sequence

in yet another contrapuntal pattern, repeated twice (mm. '9–16'). Schumann numbers the whole model and then simply reiterates it by inscribing the numerals in blank measures, leaving only his fundamental bass with some figures to remind him about harmonic progression (11ʳ, sys. 3–5).

Schumann concludes the core of the development in classic fashion by detaching a two-measure fragment from his sixteen-measure unit and continuing with the fragment in sequence until he reaches a G-major chord (11ʳ, sys. 7, m. 1). At this harmonic juncture he moves around the circle of fifths to a C-major chord which leads in turn to an F-major fermata at the top of 11ᵛ (Illustration XV; the very faint sketch at the bottom of 11ʳ seems to represent an abandoned study in developmental counterpoint rather than being attached to the preceding draft). The composer uses the fermata as the occasion for a double cadenza in keeping with a 'Spring Symphony', first a series of hunting-horn calls after the double bar and then a trill and ensuing passage-work in the treble voice at the beginning of the second system. Various notations suggest that the composer left his options open at this point, writing of a 'Variante mit Triller u[.] Flauto, Viol[ini] 1. Viol 2. Viole 2' in the upper margin. The material in this retransition provides yet another instance of gesture alluding to the first movement's introduction, with a prominent horn fanfare and leisurely cadenza used here to produce a striking rhetorical disjunction.

The composer produces the recapitulation with a series of numbers implying the exact repetition of material. The main theme begins with a new instrumentation for flutes and bassoons and a notation that the first phrase be played twice, the second time more forcefully ('bis, das 2te Mal F.'). The double bar on the seventh system and the numbers '31, 32' indicate the dramatic disjunction between the end of the main theme and the beginning of the transition. The composer fulfils the tonal requirements of the form simply by indicating the necessary point of departure for the transition ('C Moll'), after which the second theme and closing theme will follow in the tonic as a matter of course. Schumann's disjunct rhetoric throws his manipulation of sonata form as an architectonic abstraction into bolder relief, just as it did in the first movement.

The coda beginning on the middle of folio 12^r continues the process of development, compensating for the relatively short internal section of development in this draft. In fact, the composer initiates the coda with a motive from the end of the development section, and he employs a compositional device found there as well. He constructs a 26-measure unit featuring a fragment found on the bottom of 11^r, and he ends the model with an ascent to an F pedal at the bottom of 12^r (Illustration XVI). He then numbers the first eight measures of this unit '82–89' and begins a varied repetition of the whole progression on the first system of 12^v, changing the harmonies as necessary in the lower voice of each system. Schumann marks the end of the harmonic diversion with a double bar and contents himself after this point with an outline of tonic and dominant chords. These finally give way to the simple arpeggiation of a tonic chord on the last three

systems of folio 12^v, to which the composer appends a graphic
flourish with the word '*Fine*' and the date, '26 Jan. 41'.

Schumann reacted enthusiastically ('Hurrah! Symphony finished!') to this draft endowed with various qualities he had
admired in other symphonies. Absolute originality was a goal
he hardly needed to pursue after a decade of publishing highly
idiosyncratic works for piano which the larger public had for
the most part ignored. Instead Schumann created a synthesis
which followed clearly in the Beethovenian succession by virtue
of its harmonic and melodic interweaving just as it was
progressive in its adoption of Schubert's modern symphonic
style. The synthesis constitutes more than a mere obeisance to
tradition: the creation of the symphonic web endowed the piece
with structural integrity, and allusion to Schubert's 'new'
orchestral vocabulary—fashionable in Leipzig at the time—
rendered the style immediately familiar. The sketches give every
indication that Schumann wished to create a work immediately
acceptable to a wider public; the accessibility of the Spring
Symphony would be the foundation upon which he would
establish his reputation as a composer of importance.

Schumann's highly conventionalized view of form in the
continuity draft has much to do with his view of the symphony
as a particularly public genre. His larger planning in this sketch
articulates the sections of the piece with striking clarity, leaving
no doubt that he had not strayed too far from the 'middle point'
of textbook prescriptions while toying with their rearrangement.
The draft for Op. 38 is among Schumann's most carefully
calculated in its readily evident system of numbering. Invention
comes at the beginning of the sketch for each movement, while
the remainder executes a strategy. We should not be surprised
at the precision of Schumann's calculations, considering that he
had engaged over a period of years in lengthy study of the task
entailed in composition of a symphony.

Schumann composed the sketch for Op. 38 with such alacrity,
then, because he had the elements of his synthesis in mind at
the start of the exercise. The attraction in the Spring Symphony
results from the composer's marvellous combination of pre-
selected style, technique, and formal interplay. The result, if not
subtle in its larger aspects, is outgoing and ebullient, a style in
transition between the aphoristic wit of his earlier writing for

piano and the more tightly knit construction and mature tone found in his works from the later half of the decade.[35] Schumann's manipulation of content within the traditional architectonic framework suggests a clever confection meant to attract instant attention.

[35] Anthony Newcomb discusses some of the wit in the early piano pieces as well as the last movement of Op. 41, no. 3, 'Narrative Strategies', pp. 169–74.

3 Scoring of the First Version of Op. 38

In scoring the First Symphony, Schumann employed the methods he had developed for the G-minor Symphony. The process unfolded in three stages, the first of which—study of orchestral music by an admired composer—we have already glimpsed in passing. Schumann attended not only to the syntactic features of the Great C-major Symphony but also to its orchestration ('all the instruments are human voices, ingenious beyond measure, and this instrumentation quite independent of Beethoven'), thus broadening his autodidactic course in scoring and leaving Schubertian impressions on the sound of the First Symphony. The chronology for the production of this score displays the remaining stages in Schumann's process of instrumentation, including consultation with Leipzig's musicians about the initial scoring and arranging for a performance, through his influential friends and his wife. From the last stage Schumann would eventually derive revisions of his instrumentation empirically. The events of this period, like most of those for the rest of this piece, can be fixed almost to the hour by reviewing the composer's household accounts in conjunction with his correspondence and diaries.

Schumann began scoring on 27 January 1841, the day after he had completed the sketches, but in spite of his initial enthusiasm, orchestration proved more tedious than the composition of the draft. He wrote in his accounts on 1 February, 'Worked, but with great effort. I need rest.'[1] Nevertheless, he finished scoring the first movement in nine days of continuous labour on 4 February, and after only a day of respite he continued with the slow movement on the 6th and concluded on the 8th. At this point Schumann listed himself in the accounts as a 'symphony cripple'[2] and left work on the Scherzo until 12 February, finishing this movement on the next day. The

---

[1] 'Gearbeitet, doch mit Anstrengung. Es thut mir Ruhe noth.' *Haushaltbücher*, p. 173.
[2] Ibid. 174.

last movement took a moderate amount of time, five days from 15 to 20 February; its completion marks the existence of a version which would serve as the basis for further polishing (see Table 6 for a summary of the chronology of this and subsequent events).

TABLE 6 *Chronology of scoring and performance for the first version of Op. 38*

Date	Activity	Source
27 Jan.–4 Feb.	Scoring of the first movement	*Haushaltbücher*, auto.
6–8 Feb.	Scoring of the second movement	*Haushaltbücher*, auto.
12–13 Feb.	Scoring of the third movement	*Haushaltbücher*, auto.
14 Feb.	Preview of symphony for Wenzel, Pfundt	*Haushaltbücher*, diary
15–20 Feb.	Scoring of the fourth movement	*Haushaltbücher*, auto.
27 Feb.	Payment to 'copyist for symphony'	*Haushaltbücher*
1 Mar.	Begin review of score	*Haushaltbücher*
2 Mar.	Approach to Mendelssohn at Frege's (?)	*Haushaltbücher*
5 Mar.	Finish review of score	*Haushaltbücher*
6 Mar.	Takes score to Mendelssohn	*Haushaltbücher*, diary
10 Mar.	Mendelssohn invites the Schumanns to perform a benefit concert	*Haushaltbücher*, diary
11–13 Mar.	Revision of score	*Haushaltbücher*
17 Mar.	Request for violin rehearsal in message to Hilf	Erler
26 Mar.	First rehearsal of Op. 38	*Haushaltbücher*
27–30 Mar.	Revision of score	*Haushaltbücher*
31 Mar.	Morning rehearsal, evening première	*Haushaltbücher*

The relatively lengthy period devoted to the initial orchestration of Op. 38 contrasts markedly to the brief period required to sketch the piece. I have already observed some of the reasons for the brevity of sketching, including the most important: Schumann's very clear preconception of the style, technique, and form he wished to fuse in Op. 38. The sketch shows just as firm a notion of the primary orchestral colours to be used, but the technical matters of scoring—wind transpositions, instrumental ranges, and the like—probably occupied much time during the process. Schumann had already acquainted himself with the basics of these problems in his earlier orchestral attempts, but he had not developed the facility that would mark the instrumentation of his later symphonies and overtures. The question of facility aside, the time Schumann invested in scoring reveals the weight he placed upon the conception of a symphony as a work of art in which sonority forms a fundamental compositional element.

Schumann began consultation with Leipzig friends and colleagues even before he had finished his instrumentation. On 14 February, for instance, he played the symphony at the keyboard for two dinner guests, the pianist and critic Ernst Wenzel and the Gewandhaus timpanist Ernst Pfundt.[3] The preview served to enlist the sympathies of Wenzel, who would ultimately write a review of the première for the *Leipziger Zeitung*. And the composer must have sought Pfundt's technical expertise for an especially interesting timpani part involving three instead of the usual two instruments.[4] Both men could be expected to spread word of the piece around the small city of Leipzig to their many professional acquaintances. And Schumann must have wished particularly to broadcast rumours as far as Felix Mendelssohn, for the composer remembered well Mendelssohn's influential role in the publication of the the Great C-major Symphony.

Schumann arranged quite deliberately to engage Mendelssohn's advocacy. Suspecting that he would encounter his friend at a party to be given by university professor Richard Frege on 2 March, Schumann paid a copyist to set a particularly confused portion of the score in order on 27 February,[5] and he began a careful review of the polished result on 1 March. He probably mentioned the symphony to Mendelssohn in casual conversation at Frege's soirée, asking the conductor's advice as he had Müller's during the instrumentation of the G-minor Symphony.

[3] Schumann omits the final 't' in Pfundt's name, ibid. In their joint diaries Clara gives 11 February as the date for this preview, but I am inclined to believe Schumann's accounts because he kept them daily, while entries in the diaries often came a week after the fact. See Eugenie Schumann, *Robert Schumann. Ein Lebensbild meines Vaters* (Leipzig, 1931), 288.

[4] Schumann particularly admires Pfundt's playing in his accolade for the Gewandhaus printed some years earlier; see above p. 18.

[5] He records payment to 'dem Notenschreiber f.[ür] Symphonie' on 27 February, *Haushaltbücher*, p. 175. The fee most probably represents compensation for the fair copy of the exposition from the last movement that appears in the LC manuscript. See my discussion below, p. 69.

Schumann records 5 March as the date on which he completed his review, writing in the marriage diary on the following day:

Friday, the 6th, I went immediately with my score to Mendelssohn. I wanted to hear his opinion of it. What he said much astonished me. He always sees and finds the right thing. Remarkably, most of his corrections concerned the revised passages and agreed, for the most, with my first sketch. That was a penetrating review.[6]

Mendelssohn was very taken with the piece and during a visit on 10 March to the Schumanns he broached the subject of a special concert for the benefit of the Gewandhaus pension fund featuring a performance by Clara as well as Robert's symphony. Clara's reputation as a pianist during this period exceeded Robert's as a composer, and Schumann's experience with the G-minor Symphony under the guidance of Wieck had taught him to place premières on programmes with well-known virtuosos. The composer would not soon abandon the strategy for the later performances of this symphony or for the first performances of his other symphonies. The double bill featuring a talented wife and husband together possessed a certain charm of its own, naturally, but Schumann was well aware that many of the benefits derived from his wife's extraordinary fame.

Schumann set to work the day after Mendelssohn's visit on the final preparations for a performance of Op. 38. He undertook another series of revisions from 11 to 13 March, possibly based on Mendelssohn's suggestions. And he even requested a review by one of the Gewandhaus violinists, Christoph Hilf, in a letter dated 17 March 1841:

I am interested in playing through a symphony which I have composed, with a proficient fiddler, especially because it will probably be performed in the coming week, and it is always good if a few of the main supports of the orchestra know it, at least a little bit.

If you have time to come to me perhaps *Friday, at any time you wish*, do let me know. You would be doing me a real favour in this.[7]

Rehearsals began just nine days later on 26 March, and they were followed by several days worth of 'corrections',[8] another rehearsal on the morning of 31 March, and the première at the

---

[6] Eugenie Schumann, *Lebensbild*, pp. 290–1.
[7] Erler, *Briefe*, i. 257.
[8] *Haushaltbücher*, p. 178.

Gewandhaus that evening. This sequence of events marks Schumann's progress from the second stage of consultation about his orchestration to the final stage of revision by trial and error, a method that became central to his process of scoring. Long-standing friendships in Leipzig, cultivated assiduously and intensified by his work as editor of the *Neue Zeitschrift*, directly facilitated this later phase of his symphonic compositional process.

REVISIONS OF THE MUSICAL SYNTAX DURING ORCHESTRATION

Schumann followed the musical syntax of his sketches closely in the process of orchestration, making only a few minor revisions in the existing material. All such adumbrations, however, leave certain details and sometimes whole passages to be resolved during the process of writing out the score, and the sketches for Op. 38 prove no exception in this regard. The composer inserted several significant passages into the structure he had drafted previously, sometimes extending material already present in his sketch or creating entirely new material. After his initial pass through the score the composer made at least one extensive addition to the third movement of the Spring Symphony where he had a structural end in mind, but this change altered none of the material already present in his sketches.

The manuscript score for the first version of Op. 38 resides today with the preliminary drafts in the Library of Congress, ML 96.S415 Case, and its musical text appears in the composer's hand except for the exposition to the finale. This segment was recorded by Schumann's usual copyist during the period,[9] a service for which the composer disbursed four thalers on 27 February 1841 (see Table 6 above). The pages of the score, like the sketches, have been detached from their original binding and placed in transparent library paper for the sake of preservation, preventing a precise determination of the original gatherings. Two leaves, 55 and 56 (originally a bifolio?) at the end of the first movement, have been inserted during a later pass through the manuscript: we can see the hashmarks on 55^r

---

[9] Schumann's only named copyist from this period is C. Brückner; see my discussion of the engraver's manuscript in ch. 5.

and 57ʳ that usually signify such additions in Schumann's
autographs, as well as the composer's original sequence of page
numbers which jumps from '82' on 54ᵛ to '83' on 57ʳ. Folio 58
contains a completely unrelated fragmentary setting of Psalm 13
('Herr, Herr, hast du mich ganz vergeßen? Wie lange verbirgst
du dein Antlitz von mir?')[10] for a quartet of voices; the leaf
may simply be the second half of a scrap bifolio which the
composer used for the last few measures of the first movement.
And finally, Kinsky tells us that the two concluding leaves (left
unnumbered) containing much of the text for the second trio
did not appear as part of the original binding, but were added
in 1909.[11] The manuscript in the Library of Congress also
preserves a small number of fragments originally pasted over
portion of full folios; the inserts are now bound individually
and interleaved with the appropriate pages of the autograph
(they appear at the very end of the Lehman facsimile).

Schumann occasionally adjusted the structural balance during
orchestration by extending material already present in his sketch;
the best example comes in the development section of the first
movement. The bridge just prior to the retransition appears as
a segment of twenty measures (counting the specified repetitions
6ʳ, systems 2–4) in the original adumbration, featuring a series
of rising chromatic scales in dotted rhythms followed by
blank measures representing modulatory chords. The composer
indicates in his draft that he means to repeat his basic unit, and
in fact his score begins with an eight-measure model and its
sequence (35ʳ–36ʳ, mm. '210–17' [*246–53*][12] and '218–25' [*254–
61*]), each made from four measures (2 x 2) of rising scales in
dotted rhythms and four measures of shifting harmonies (see
Table 7 for a schematic of this section). The sketch provides no
other music here, but Schumann sees a chance to accelerate the
tonal motion by detaching a fragment of the scalar material for

---

[10] 'How long wilt thou forget me, O Lord? for ever? How long wilt thou hide thy
face from me?' Kinsky misreads this text as 'Herr, Herr, hast Du mich ganz verlaßen?',
imagining a setting of Psalm 22, *Musikhistorisches Museum von Wilhelm Heyer in Cöln*,
iv. 344.

[11] Ibid. 342.

[12] The measure numbers in quotations are Schumann's; they appear during this
passage in the bottom margin of each page. Both foliation and numbering can be seen
in the printed facsimile, Schumann, *Symphony Opus 38* (New York, 1967). Measure
numbers in italics refer to the corresponding passages in the final version.

TABLE 7. *Structure of bridge 2 in first movement autograph of Op. 38*

Phrase	Folio	Pitch level	Schumann's Nos.	Score mm.
Model	35^{r-v}	E^b	'210–17'	246–253
Sequence	35^v–36^r	D	'218–25'	254–261
Fragment	36^{r-v}	C	'226–29'	262–265
repeated	36^v	D	'230–33'	266–269
repeated	37^r	E^b	'234–37'	270–273
repeated	37^{r-v}	D	'238–41'	274–277
repeated	37^v	C	'242–45'	278–281
Harm. prep.	38^r	A$^{°4/2}$–G^b Ger.$^{+6}$	'246–53'	282–289

sequential display in 4-measure units with antiphonal responses between strings and woodwinds. The final sequence, for violins alone (mm. '242–5' [*278–81*]), ultimately leads the composer back to his sketched conception of an augmented sixth chord on G flat resolving to the F pedal for the grand return of the opening motto. The insertion not only adds to the proportions of the development, it also prepares a more dramatic entrance of the fanfare by accelerating toward the harmonic fulcrum of the movement. Here the F sharp from the key of D major, respelled in most (but not all) voices as G flat, resolves emphatically down to F, returning the listener to the ambitus of B-flat major. At this juncture we begin to understand Schumann's indecision about the pitch of the third timpano, F sharp on the first page of sketching but G flat in the score, and we see some of the harmonic tension engendered by the prominent use of D major in this piece. Schumann apparently extends this passage without the aid of a special draft, merely by manipulating the material already at hand.

The appearance of a coda at the end of the first movement in the autograph presents a more complicated instance of extension in which Schumann combines pre-existent ideas from his fragmentary sketch on folio 7^r with new material. The new music for the coda (which replaces the closing material after the second transition) appears first in the form of a four-measure unit derived logically enough from the head motive of the main theme (45^r, 'Molto piu Allegro' [mm. *381–3*]; see Table 8) repeated in rising sequence four times. Schumann concludes with

TABLE 8. *Structure of the first movement coda in the autograph of Op. 38*

Phrase	Derivation	Location	Score mm.
a	Main theme, second transition	45^r, m. 5–47^r	381–404
a′		47^v–49^r	405–428
Bridge 1	New cadences	49^v–50^r, m. 1	429–437
b	New lyrical interlude	50^r, m. 2–50^v, m. 7	438–451
b′		50^v, m. 8–51^v	452–467
Bridge 2	New cadences	52^r–53^r, m. 1	468–483
Final cadences	Sketch, 7^r	53^r, m. 2–57^r	484–515

a two-measure unit derived from material in the second transition repeated four times, followed by a cadence in B flat (46^v, m. 3 to the end of 47^r [mm. *396–404*]). He continues merely by reiterating this whole unit transposed an octave higher, adding to the end an extended cadential section dwelling on a dominant chord (49^v [mm. *429–37*]). The next segment involves a lyrical theme seemingly unrelated to the rest of the movement,[13] played first in the strings (50^{r-v}, m. 7 [mm. *438–51*]) and then repeated with the addition of winds (mm. *452–67*). A short fragment from the beginning of this lyrical theme repeats to form a bridge (f. 52 [mm. *468–83*]) to the concluding cadential figures, which derive from the brief sketches on 7^r (see above, Ex. 2.7). Schumann originally writes a short series of cadential chords moving directly from 54^v to the conclusion on 57^r. During one of the many later reviews before the performance on 31 March, the composer decides that the cadential area needs more length, and he adds two folios to the manuscript.[14] He first specifies in pencil a repeat of measures 2 to 8 from 54^v ('die vorhergehenden

---

[13] The idea may, in fact, derive from the scalar answer to the opening motto in the introduction, but the resemblance is distant at best.

[14] I deduce the chronology from circumstantial evidence. The paper for this insertion is identical to that in the remainder of the first movement, but the use of pencil, the medium for most of Schumann's corrections to a text written initially in ink, strongly suggests that the addition occurred at least after the movement had been completed, and possibly after the completion of the rest of the manuscript. By the same token, Schumann must have inserted this revision before the writing of the second trio which appears on a new variety of paper. And since the second trio was heard at the first performance, the revised closing for the coda on the earlier paper must predate the première.

7 Tacte noch einmal' [mm. *495–501*]), adds a series of stereotypical tonic-dominant alternations (mm. *503–7*), and finally appends a rising arpeggiation of a B-flat major chord in half notes on 55ᵛ to 56ʳ (mm. *508–10*). Only then does he turn to 57ʳ (mm. *511–15*), where he lengthens the duration of these chords from quarter notes to half notes.

Given the simplicity of the phrase structure in this coda and the substantial revisions Schumann makes early in its history, it seems likely that the composer produced it in score without reference to a complete continuity draft. The melodic units usually repeat in pairs, and the passage involves harmonic progressions seen earlier in the course of the first movement. Two brief sketches containing ideas, a few measures for the first pair of phrases and a few more for the lyrical interlude, could have been drafted and linked to the fragment on 7ᵛ during orchestration. This casual method of construction would help explain why major details like the proportion of the cadential close and even the time signature and barring[15] on 53ᵛ required later adjustment.

The notion that Schumann constructed this coda during orchestration by linking three isolated short drafts would also account for its independence. Apart from the material taken from the main theme at the beginning, this conclusion appears independent of the movement. It serves as an ending of suitable weight, but the lyrical interlude interrupts forward motion before the closing cadences. The language of the first movement as a whole often involves detachment occasioned by reversals, but nowhere else does the dramatic rhetoric result in this degree of separation.

While Schumann leaves at least some hint in his sketches about his desire for a coda for the first movement, he gives no inkling about the addition of a completely new trio to the third movement. But this new material seems less disturbing to the integrity of the piece, simply because a trio consitutes by definition a distinct, contrasting entity in a larger movement. We do not know exactly when the idea of a second trio occurred to Schumann. But we can tell at least that it came after he had finished his initial scoring of the symphony on 20 February, for

---

15 Schumann's note, '*Allabreve Tact* vorzuzeichnen' ('bar in alla breve time'), refers to the change between 2/4 and 4/4 time.

this music does not appear on the same paper as the rest of the manuscript, nor was it stored originally with the rest of the leaves. On the other hand, accounts of the première discuss the second trio, which must have been completed before 31 March.[16]

The melodic idea of the trio is quite plain: the main theme, presented in a first strain of eight measures, consists of a two-measure ascending scale offered three times in imitation (in the basses, the violas, and then the violins) and closed by a two-measure cadential progression (see Ex. 3.1). The composer develops this motive in the second strain by employing its inverted form and exploring its potential for counterpoint. Because the material is so simple, we can easily imagine that the first strain could have been written without the aid of a sketch. The creation of the second strain probably required just a brief draft (now lost to us) resolving some of the contrapuntal difficulties.[17]

The lack of a distinctive melody in the second trio suggests that Schumann is more interested in its tonal import. Cast in B-flat major, the second trio recalls the primary tonal focus of the symphony during a movement devoted largely to D minor

Example 3.1   Schumann, Op. 38, mvt. 4, excerpt from beginning of Trio II in reduction

---

[16] See, for instance, '*Leipzig*. (Beschluss)', *AMZ* xliii (1841), col. 331.

[17] Schumann often contemplated contrapuntal arrangements in brief trial sketches, like the one discussed by Rufus Hallmark in 'A Sketch Leaf for Schumann's D-Minor Symphony', *Mendelssohn and Schumann: Essays on Their Music and Its Context*, ed. Jon W. Finson and R. Larry Todd (Durham, NC, 1984), 39–51.

(the scherzo proper) and D major (the first trio). The composer's concentration on the dominant pitch of F in the second trio— it opens the first strain and concludes the second, though Schumann attaches a coda to cadence finally on B flat—completes the plan first outlined in the exposition of the first movement, in which various themes articulate B flat, its mediant of D, and finally its dominant. With the new addition, the various parts of the third movement take on a consistent pattern of function, with the scherzo proper developing melodic material from the second movement, while the two trios emphasize motivic and tonal aspects of the first movement.

Apart from the larger additions that affect the proportion and structure of the piece, Schumann also indulges in a series of smaller scale melodic revisions in the musical fabric during instrumentation. It would be difficult to recount all these, but we can examine the most significant. The composer revises the main theme of the first movement by transposing the head motive from a beginning on D to an initiation on B flat (the divisi flutes unify to a single pitch in Ex. 3.2), reflecting his alteration of the opening motto in the introduction during the process of sketching.[18] He adjusts the main theme in the exposition of the finale by repeating the first four measures (82^v– 83^r) to make it resemble the parallel passage in the recapitulation (f. 97 [mm. *174–81*]) (in the sketch only the recapitulation had featured this reiteration). And finally, Schumann decides about some details left open in the sketches, whether, for instance, the retransition in the final movement should feature another flute cadenza or the 'Variant with trills' suggested in the adumbration (11^v). In this case he chooses to avoid the redundancy of a second flute cadenza, selecting the proposed variant instead (96^v–97^r). Schumann regards most of these revisions as essentially superficial,

Example 3.2   Schumann, Op. 38, mvt. 1, excerpt from autograph of altered flute parts for main theme

---

[18] See my discussion of this revision in the sketches, pp. 36–7.

the result of polishing for the sake of consistency or for variety. He often alters these same passages again in later versions, returning to his original conception.

ORCHESTRAL STYLE IN THE FIRST VERSION OF OP. 38

Schumann chose a relatively large and occasionally exotic orchestra for the Spring Symphony, viewed in the context of Leipzig during the mid-nineteenth century. On the first page of sketches he specifies three timpani in F, F sharp, and B flat, (two) trumpets in B flat, (two) horns in F, (two) horns in B flat, (two) clarinets in B flat, (two) oboes, (two) flutes, (two) bassoons, bass trombone, and he simply assumes the usual string choir.[19] The autograph adds to this assemblage (14^r) the remaining two trombones, a triangle, and plans (left unrealized) for a harp in the second movement (59^r). The Gewandhaus ensemble of 1841 featured, as we have seen earlier, nine first violins, eight seconds, five violas, five cellos, four basses, and two each of the usual woodwinds, horns, and trumpets.[20] The trombonists and extra horn players for Schumann's scoring seem to have been kept on permanent retainer by the orchestra; the harpist and triangle player would be engaged specially, and the timpanist would require an extra drum. This selection was ambitious but not unprecedented. Beethoven had used four horns in his Ninth Symphony, and in his treatise on orchestration Graßner explains around 1842 that this expanded practice appears in scores with increasing frequency.[21] Beethoven had also used trombones (albeit in limited fashion) in his Fifth, Sixth, and Ninth Symphonies, as had Schubert (much more prominently) in his Great C-major Symphony. If Schumann's palette was not original, the composer does work with the widest assemblage

[19] These designations appear in pencil at the top of 4^r, where they have been partially trimmed. They read in order: 'Timp. 3 in F, Fis, B. Trombe in B. Corni in F. Corni in B. Clarinetti [in] B. Oboi. Flauti. Fagotti. Trombone basso.'

[20] Dörffel, *Geschichte der Gewandhausconcerte zu Leipzig vom 25. November 1781 bis 25. November 1881* (Leipzig, 1884), i. 128.

[21] Ferdinand Simon Graßner, *Partiturkenntniß, ein Leitfaden zum Selbstunterrichte für angehende Tonsetzer, oder solche, welche Arrangiren, Partiturlesen lernen oder sich zu Dirigenten von Orchestern oder Militärmusiken bilden wollen*, 2nd edn. (Karlsruhe, 1842), i. 27.

available to German orchestration of his time none the less. The large changes in German instrumentation wrought slightly later by Liszt (when he scored his own work) and Wagner come as a result of their contact with the music of French operas and the writing of Hector Berlioz. Schumann did not hear any orchestral music by Berlioz until the composer's visit in 1843, and he seems never to have read Berlioz's treatise on instrumentation, which postdates the first edition of Op. 38 at any rate. He selects his scoring on the basis of the works he knew by earlier German symphonists, instructing himself by example and later by trial and error.

Nowhere can we see Schumann's autodidactic position so clearly as in the layout of his score in the autograph, subsequent manuscripts, and orchestral prints. The normal disposition of parts in German symphonic scores during Schumann's time follows a practice similar though not invariably the same as ours. Many scores, printed and manuscript, place the woodwinds at the top of the page, followed by the horns, trumpets, trombones, timpani, and strings, in the manner of most modern scores. Graßner, following a slightly different tradition, places the flutes, oboes, clarinets, horns, and bassoons at the top of the score (with bassoons grouped as the foundation of the woodwind quintet), the trumpets, trombones, and the timpani as 'Füllstimmen' in the middle, and the strings at the bottom of the page.[22] This arrangement can be found in printed scores from the period, including works by Lachner and Spohr, composers whom Schumann admired and whose orchestral works he knew. Schumann, however, groups the percussion, trumpets, and horns at the top of his score, then the woodwinds, the trombones, and the strings. The pairing of trumpets and timpani is traditional, and the composer generally uses these instruments in the time-honoured way, to punctuate the rhythms of heavier passages. I suspect that the 'filler voices' appear at the top of the page with the more melodically oriented horns because these parts can only play limited pitches and require special attention for this reason. The composer places instruments that can always play complete diatonic scales below the more limited brass and timpani. He follows this order in his remaining symphonic autographs, except for the manuscript of Op. 97 which exhibits

[22] Ibid. 70.

what we would call modern disposition, though the printed score displays his older habit.

Schumann's relatively extensive palette reflects his intention to elicit the most massive sonority available from the Gewandhaus ensemble of 49 players, and he accomplishes this richness of sound by a variety of means. The density of this orchestration results from the manner in which the composer imagines orchestral colour in his sketch and from the way in which he transforms this plan into a score. If the sketch largely spins the melodic thread of the piece, Schumann generally devotes only one hue to each melody. Assignments usually appear for individual instruments—melodies given to the violins alone, the flutes alone, and so forth—and the contrapuntal working in the bass also bears just one instrumental designation. The composer transfers this vision, slightly reworked, to his first pass through the autograph manuscript. Where the sketched melody appears in a single upper part, as it does for the D-major reprise of the main theme in the first movement (5^v, sys. 3), Schumann gives it mainly to one instrument, the flute in an upper register without doubling support in the score (29^r–31^r [mm. *178–93*]). The composer repeats in the score the active violin figuration indicated by the preliminary draft and the remaining voices supply harmonic support. Another example of this texture appears in the middle variation of the second movement (sketch: 8^r, sys. 5–6; transferred to score: 62^r–63^r [mm. *41–55*]), this time with the melody in the cello. Where Schumann chooses to double the melodic line in his score (for instance, in theme for the scherzo, 71^v [mm. *9–16* in the final version] or the main theme of the fourth movement, 82^v–83^r; measures in the final version do not correspond), he often adds only one other instrument, most frequently pairing the first flute with violins, or flute and oboe.

Schumann's tendency to underemphasize melodic lines in his first pass through the autograph finds its complement in his dealings with the accompaniment. Because he doubles melodic lines lightly, the composer has quite a number of instruments available for supporting roles. He creates his full orchestral sonority throughout the autograph initially by means of pervasive and redundant doublings in parts playing extended chords to support rhythmically active lines. A good example can be found in the development of the first movement (36^r to 37^v [mm. *262–81*]) where the dotted melodic parts, often carried by just the first violins or the combined basses, cellos, and bassoons, unfold over a series of suspensions carried in the remaining brass, woodwinds, and strings. A similar passage can also be found in the development section from the finale, where the brass and woodwinds play extended chords to accompany the melody in the strings (92^r–94^v [mm. *116–48*]). Winds arranged in this way take on the aspect of an amply registered organ sounding a slowly moving chorale, and Schumann's choice of a large orchestra further enhances the effect. The presence of paired horns in different transpositions, for instance, allows the composer to employ this timbre almost continually in any key. In the autograph they are rarely absent, sometimes doubling accompanimental lines in the cello and viola or providing sustained harmonic backgrounds, as in the elegaic passage from the coda to the first movement (49^v–51^v [mm.*438–67*]). The density of Schumann's scoring, then, originates in his liberal use of instruments to accompany melodic lines.

Schumann's general disposition towards dark colours and narrow spacing increases the full texture inherent in his method of transferring ideas from sketch to score. He seems to prefer the oboe (and less frequently the clarinet) to the flute for featured woodwind melodies, as in the second variation from the slow movement (65^v–67^v [mm. *78–93*]) where oboe and French horn carry the theme supported by clarinets, bassoons, and highly active strings. In this case Schumann specifically considers a flute on 66^v but deletes it, just as he does in the second theme from the first movement, given to the clarinets and bassoons when the flute and strings are removed (21^v–22^r [mm. *80–8*]). Where he uses many instruments together for support, even in brilliant passages such as the opening fanfare from the last movement (82^r), he spaces the harmonies closely and frequently places woodwinds and strings (with the first and second violins playing double stops) on the same pitch in the same octave. This style of scoring appears in the main theme of the scherzo proper (71^v), the main theme from the first movement (18^v–19^v [mm. *39–54*]), and countless other passages. Much of the writing aims to elicit a large sound from a small orchestra.

Schumann adapts many devices from the Great C-major

Symphony in pursuit of this general desire to achieve massive sonorities and seems to find Schubert's use of strings particularly remarkable. Schubert derives a great deal of sound from a small string section by re-articulation of doubled pitches, as in measures 228 to 239 from the first movement or measures 333 to 349 from the fourth movement of the C-major Symphony. While the winds present the various lines in straightforward rhythms during these tutti passages, the strings break almost every pitch into repeated eight notes, responding to the inequities of balance caused by increasing number of wind instruments, particularly brass, in the German orchestra during the first half of the nineteenth century. Re-articulation in the strings during climactic passages not only seeks to repair the imbalance, it also creates a richer texture overall. Schumann adopts this as one of his favourite devices for passages like the retransition from the first movement (39^v–40^r [mm. *290–316*]) or the second theme from the finale (f. 89 [mm. *82–96*]). The last example runs parallel to Schubert in every way: all the orchestral forces are engaged, the strings doubling the winds with pitches reiterated in eighth notes.[23]

Schumann, with the sound of the C-major Symphony still in his ears, also shows a general inclination toward active string accompaniments, like the murmurous string figurations in the second movement of Op. 38 and ornamental triplets during the reprise of the second strain in the first trio.[24] In fact, at least one such string accompaniment in Op. 38 constitutes a direct reference to the orchestration (and the material, as I have mentioned earlier) of the Great C-major Symphony. In his review of Schubert's first movement introduction Schumann explicitly admires the gentle acceleration between introduction and exposition, and he notes the basic method. Schubert had done little more than prolong a dominant chord (beginning in m. 70), add instruments to make a crescendo, and employ repetitive violin triplets to measure the beat and lend a sense of increased acitivity and sonority to the texture. Schumann initially

---

[23] Beethoven sometimes employs his orchestra in this manner, for instance in the Fourth Symphony, mvt. I, mm. 19 ff. of the allegro. But he most often uses eighth-note articulations when the strings act in purely harmonic capacities. In the Schubert C-major the texture almost becomes a trademark.

[24] Schumann's note reads, 'NB. bei der Wiederholung hat die Bratsche wie unten steht' ('NB. during the reprise, the viola has what stands below'), 75^v.

borrows the general concept of this passage but not its specific detail: he sketches the gradually accelerating arpeggiations for the strings in his introduction as a series of eighth notes (4^r, sys. 5–6), and he executes this design in the first layer of the autograph (17^r [mm. *25* ff.]). But he returns during one of his revisions to change all the even eighth notes to eighth-note triplets, gaining Schubert's rhythmic ease and fluidity in addition to his active sonority.

In his scoring for the Spring Symphony Schumann also adopts Schubert's use of trombones as prominent melodic instruments. Schubert was more fond of trombone sonorities than, say, Beethoven who uses them mostly to double chords or punctuations; and in the Great C-major Symphony he sometimes employs the trombones to articulate a slowly moving melody over ostinato-like figures in the strings and woodwinds (see the first movement, mm. 200–27). The trombones possess a two-fold virtue in such situations: as brass instruments they can produce the substantial crescendo Schubert requires, and they can play all the notes of the scale in this lower register, unlike the horns. Schumann uses the trombones in much the same way during the coda to his fourth movement (f. 105 [mm. *302–7*]); they even play rhythmic motives reminiscent of the Great C-major Symphony, though they are arranged divisi over accompanying chords rather than in unison over repeated figures. Schumann selects trombones for some of the most special moments in the autograph of the Spring Symphony, like the transition between the second and third movements (f. 70).

Finally, Schumann takes a hint from Schubert's use of pizzicato strings to articulate woodwind chords percussively. Returning again to measures 200–12 from the first movement of the Great C-major Symphony, the accompanimental figures are executed by alternating combinations of woodwind pairs (i.e. the flutes with oboes, or the clarinets with the bassoons), doubled by plucked violins or basses, respectively. Schumann utilizes the plucked upper strings to double various combinations of woodwinds with truly striking results in the last movement of Op. 38 at the beginning of the transition (86^r [mm. *43* ff.]). In this instance, Schumann has made creative use of his model by featuring the combination in a prominent melodic role where Schubert employs it as a background effect. Schumann's emulation of Schubert does not involve slavish imitation; rather he adapts attractive sounds that lead him closer to the rich and varied sonority he envisions for the symphony.

Schumann employs a variety of techniques to achieve his vision of a lush and powerful orchestral sound in this autograph. His use of Schubertian devices for dealing with strings and certain winds aids him in this attempt, as do his redundant doublings of supporting harmonic voices, his close spacing of chords, and his preference for more sombre instrumental colours in the middle ranges. We should not be too surprised to discover Schumann's fondness for closely spaced parts in the middle registers, since his piano writing reveals this same preference for sonorities formed in the central portion of the keyboard. But this general conception of sound applied to orchestral music creates something quite original: no matter how much Schumann borrows isolated techniques from one composer or another, his synthesis in the first pass through the autograph yields an entirely distinctive and potent texture.

SCHUMANN'S REVISION OF SCORING IN THE MANUSCRIPT OF THE FIRST VERSION

While Schumann clearly desired a massive orchestral sonority, he saw immediately that he would need to rethink some of his initial means for realizing his aural image. The evidence of his dissatisfaction with the first pass through the score of Op. 38 is strewn over almost every page in the form of copious revisions. Some of this reworking occurred even as the piece was orchestrated initially and some during the several reviews of the autograph Schumann mentions in his diaries before the première on 31 March (see Table 6). These later re-examinations occasioned a large number of pencilled queries in the margins of the first version, and corrections to the musical text in both pencil and ink resulted from the later passes as well. We cannot possibly examine all of Schumann's many alterations here, but we can view a number of representative examples.

Many of the composer's queries and reminders were destroyed when the margins were trimmed for the original binding, but those that survive give a good sense of Schumann's concerns.

He often muses over details of figuration in the margins, questioning the writing for the violas during the second theme in the first movement on 21^v and 22^r, the violins during the development section on 29^r, or the violins and violas in the beginning of the second movement, 59^r. The composer also devotes a good deal of attention to reviewing wind doublings, as the frequent queries in the margin testify. He writes, for instance, in the second movement at the first transition 'trombe ? nicht mit' (63^r), in the second variation at the onset of the melody 'vielleicht[?] 3 Hörner und[?] 1stes Hoboe.' (65^v), or in the transition to the third movement, 'Fagotti ? nicht zu schwach' (70^r). Such queries also appear in the exposition of the fourth movement, even though the copyist presumably enters a version of this passage rewritten to incorporate most earlier corrections. Schumann apparently does not regard the orchestration as perfected in any stage of this manuscript.

Many of the revisions in the autograph display Schumann's concern that he had used his ensemble too monotonously. His solutions to such problems often came immediately during his first attempt at a passage. For instance, Schumann originally scores the second theme in the first movement for flutes and strings (21^v–22^r [mm. *81–8*]), but finding this sound too bright and the scoring too heavy for his tastes, he deletes the flutes, violins, and cellos. The composer gives the theme instead to the clarinets and bassoons, leaving a pattern of accompanimental sixteenth notes in the viola part. The passage in its second state is not only clearer, it has the virtue of contrast with the surrounding music. The sketches suggest that Schumann makes this change as he realizes the adumbration in score, for the original pencilled assignment of the melody to the violins (4^v) is deleted in the ink of the score, with the reassignment to oboe, clarinet, and bassoon also in ink. The score provides further evidence that this change comes early in the process of orchestration: the section appears in the recapitulation (42^v [mm. *344–51*]) without any visible corrections (here it features the oboe on the melodic line rather than the clarinet), implying that Schumann has established his aural image of the passage by this point and therefore proceeds without hesitation. The recapitulation in the first movement contains relatively few revisions because Schumann has already arrived at his scoring of a given passage in the exposition and generally follows a similar course for the formal repetition. The manuscript of the last movement suggests this same process indirectly, for only the exposition apparently stood in need of a copyist before the first performance, while the composer preserves his own first pass through the recapitulation (corrected, of course). Schumann's tendency to repeat his instrumentation of an exposition for its formal repetition re-emphasizes his relatively abstract view of structure during this period.

Schumann often realizes in the course of revision that he has overdone his scoring of accompaniment in his attempt to derive a large symphonic sound from a small orchestra. In these situations he reduces doublings and seeks to clarify accompanimental figuration, as we can see at the beginning of the second movement. The composer originally gives the melody here to the first violins divided at the octave, doubled by the first clarinet in the lower range (59^r, Ex. 3.3). The horns, second clarinet, bassoons, violas, cellos, and basses provide the accompaniment. In his revision, Schumann removes all the woodwinds and horns, deletes the upper octave in the first violins, and changes the figuration in the lower strings. Instead of parallel thirds played by the violas, he substitutes a pattern of mildly syncopated eighth and sixteenth notes, retaining the thirty-second-note motion in a lighter version for the second violins (Schumann begins to enter this revision in pencil on the second violin line and then moves to a line left blank by the abandoned harp; see Ex. 3.4). Both of his revisions reduce the texture of the main theme for the sake of contrast with the last variation, where the woodwinds and horns will inherit the melody over a more active figuration in the strings (65^v).

Schumann's preference for full texture becomes particularly problematic when he indulges in static chordal accompaniments, and these situations often elicit some sort of alteration. In the first layer of the coda to the Scherzo, for instance (Ex. 3.5a), Schumann gives the melody to the first flute doubled by the clarinets, with an answer in the first bassoon punctuated by the lower horns and trumpets. The timpani, horns in D, oboes, second bassoon, and upper four strings hold chords. In the second layer of the passage (Ex. 3.5b), Schumann apparently finds the melodic lines too weak and the accompaniment too

Example 3.3   Schumann, Op. 38, mvt. 2, first layer of scoring for main theme in autograph

Example 3.4   Schumann, Op. 38, mvt. 2, revised figuration for second violins, violas in autograph

heavy. He reinforces the flute with the first violins and the first bassoon with the cellos, gives the second bassoon a more interesting line in conjunction with the violas, and assigns the clarinets a harmonic role. The composer then provides rests in many of the other parts to reduce the pervasive quality of the accompaniment. The result articulates the melodic and contrapuntal lines more clearly, creates greater contrast between the upper and lower registers, and also lends more rhythmic vitality to this passage. The texture remains heavy due to the horn and timpani as well as to the many doublings in the same octave.

Schumann also makes a few technical miscalculations in his attempt to elicit full sonorities from a small ensemble. He over-indulges his passion for rearticulated string melodies in the coda of the last movement, where he initially writes a tremolo (103ʳ [mm. *277* ff.]) before realizing that it is ineffectual at this very fast pace. Though he does not renounce the device entirely, he reduces the speed of the thirty-second notes to sixteenths by writing, 'NB. In all string instruments only 16ths from here to the close.'[25] Perhaps the best example of technical problems in his writing for strings can be seen at the beginning of the exposition from the first movement. Schumann originally follows his sketch for this passage, beginning the melody in D and scoring it for flute (see above Ex. 3.2) and first violins playing multiple stops (Ex. 3.6*a*). At the same time he changes the beginning pitch to B flat; the composer also sees that the violins and violas will have difficulty executing their multiple stops at

25 'NB. In allen Streichinstrumenten nur *16*thele von hier bis zum Schluss.'

a quick tempo, for he revises the rhythm of the violin parts, using them to punctuate beats, and reduces the violas to a unison pitch (Ex. 3.6*b*). The alteration represents an improvement though it still leaves a relatively thick texture. Passages posing such technical problems for the strings were probably the occasion for Christoph Hilf's consultation with the composer.

Expert advice did not help in avoiding another technical miscalculation which became apparent at the first rehearsal. Schumann reminds his adviser, Mendelssohn, on the occasion of an 1845 performance of Op. 38: 'You may well be in the middle of my symphony! Do you still remember the first rehearsal in the year 1841—and the stopped trumpets and horns at the beginning? It really sounded like sneezing; I must laugh when I think about it.'[26] This statement refers to the opening motto, scored in Schumann's autograph for natural trumpets and horns in B flat (he had mistakenly entered the motto for the first and second horns as well, but immediately realized he had chosen the wrong line and blotted the pitches before the ink dried). The tonic pitch of B flat will play perfectly on the natural instruments, but in order to obtain G and A, the player must alter the length of the air column by stopping the bell with his hand. The effect resembles the use of a mute on a modern horn, resulting in Schumann's comparison to sneezing. This phenomenon marks all music written for natural brasses, and it can be heard very clearly in recordings, for example, of the trio to the third movement of Beethoven's Third Symphony played on natural horns.[27] In a very quick tempo the stopped notes do not disturb the listener, but in Schumann's introduction with its sustained pitches the effect is intolerable.

We know by hearsay Schumann's solution to the problem of the stopped horns at the first rehearsal: he returned to his initial conception of the gesture in his sketches with the opening pitch on D.[28] We must suppose that he entered this revision in the individual parts, but not in the autograph. Technical miscalculations like this one sometimes lead to the stories of Schumann's incompetence in instrumentation, but during his

[26] Jansen, *Briefe*, p. 251.

[27] See Ludwig van Beethoven, *Sinfonie Nr. 3, Es*-dur, *Op. 55*, perf. Collegium Aureum (Deutsche Harmonia Mundi, matrix no. IC 065–99–629 QB, 1976).

[28] Jansen, *Briefe*, p. 518, n. 321.

Example 3.5*a* Schumann, Op. 38, mvt. 3, original scoring for beginning of coda in autograph

Example 3.5*b* Schumann, Op. 38, mvt. 3, revised scoring for beginning of coda in autograph

Example 3.6*a*   Schumann, Op. 38, mvt. 1, original scoring of strings
for main theme in autograph

Example 3.6*b*   Schumann, Op. 38, mvt. 1, revised scoring of strings
for main theme in autograph

inspections of the score even Mendelssohn failed to note the
consequences of Schumann's fanfare in its first version.

Schumann's failure to enter this change in his manuscript score
suggests that some of the revisions made between the first
rehearsal on 26 March 1841 and the performance on 31 March
appear only in the individual parts now lost to us. The missing
horn correction also implies that the autograph presents an
arrested state of the piece as it appeared in late March 1841. The
version printed later in 1841 differs significantly in both major
and minor details for which the LC autograph provides no
prehistory. We can see from the manuscript that Schumann
initially creates a piece with a rich and full scoring and
immediately identifies the attendant disadvantage of his aural
image. Too much emphasis on massive sonority in accom-

panimental lines tends to obscure the more delicately scored melody in the first layers of the autograph. Schumann begins to rectify this imbalance by removing some of the accompaniment while reinforcing the melodic writing. But the process remained incomplete because Schumann had not yet received the full benefit of the third, empirical stage in his method of orchestration; he had heard his piece in only a limited number of rehearsals by 31 March. The autograph in the Library of Congress shows a complete and performable version which served as a resting place on the way to the final product.

RECEPTION OF THE PREMIÈRE

A great deal of anticipation surrounded the extra concert at the Gewandhaus which featured Clara playing excerpts from Chopin's Second Piano Concerto and pieces by Schumann, Mendelssohn, and Scarlatti amidst the usual vocal selections. Dörffel, an eyewitness to the event, prefaces his account with an assessment of the atmosphere:

Clara Schumann . . . had announced a concert for 31 March, which programme contained a composition at the beginning of the second part designated plainly and simply 'Symphony by R. Schumann'. Symphony by R. Schumann? Many questioned in this manner and displayed great astonishment that Schumann had written a symphony. Very few had heeded the piano pieces and collections of songs that had been published by Schumann up to that time, and Schumann was completely unfamiliar as a composer to orchestral musicians and to the public. Even as editor of the Neue Zeitschrift für Musik he had by no means made much impression on the public.[29]

Mendelssohn held three rehearsals of the symphony and spared no pains to ensure the best possible rendition, and his devotion yielded results:

The performance of the symphony proceeded brilliantly. The listeners became extraordinarily excited by the work, though at first much affected them negatively, so that one could not say that the reception had been entirely splendid. After the second movement, the *Larghetto*, under the influence of the trombones which were unexpectedly heard

[29] Dörffel, *Geschichte*, i. 96.

at the close like the distant tones of an organ sounding afar from a house of worship, the same solemn hush fell that has probably not been missing from any performance since; after the Scherzo, which closed like an unanswered question, dying away *pianissimo* like the larghetto movement, still no applause followed: most believed the real conclusion had not come. Against this, the uproarious tones of the woodwinds (the oboes at first with the bassoons, then with the clarinets) in conjunction with the pizzicato of the violins and violas struck with such vigour after the main theme in the finale, that many in the back of the hall arose to see what was transpiring in the orchestra to engender such remarkable sonorous effects. In short, [the audience] was quite singularly moved in many respects. Still, in the orchestra itself they couldn't always find their way into the spirit of the work by any means. Almost every instrument had a ticklish passage which was difficult to perform at that time and impaired the players' appreciation of the whole. Specifically, the second violins were preoccupied with the approach that could best bring out the figures in the main theme of the finale; these were piano, not violin passages, they said, sulking somewhat. Even the flautist Grenser who otherwise did not have anything against a challenge, resisted the well-known cadenza in the finale a bit. Only Pfundt was completely satisfied that the composer had 'written in' an exceptional three timpani instead of two. In the end, the success with all of these was such that Schumann was seen in a different light from then on and respected to a much greater degree than previously. The symphony had far exceeded all expectations, then.[30]

The enthusiastic reaction to Schumann's full orchestration re-sounds in every review. Wenzel, for whom the composer had already previewed the piece on piano, writes with renewed delight in the *Leipziger Zeitung*:

Apart from [Clara's] feats, however, the compositions by Robert Schumann commanded the most widespread interest. A symphony by him surprised [us] by its lively freshness and purity of ideas no less than by the great power of its instrumentation and its beautiful orchestral effects, and [it] may be regarded as a joyful herald announcing a rich future for this composer.[31]

[30] Dörffel, ibid.

[31] Ibid. 214; Schumann resented Wenzel's 'surprise' and objected to the journalistic habit of referring to a composer's future rather than appraising the worth of the piece under consideration; see Jansen, *Briefe*, p. 205.

The *AMZ* also expressed delighted surprise that the piece was 'knowledgeably, tastefully, and often quite successfully and effectively orchestrated'.[32]

The critics at the concert immediately understood the meaning of the piece and the significance of its musical language and gesture. The anonymous critic for the *AMZ* observed that the first movement begins 'unisono' like the Great C-major and noted the 'reminiscences of Franz Schubert resounding throughout', assessing Schumann's emulation in unmistakable terms:

The first works of an artist, even the initial pieces of our principal artistic heroes, have never laid claim and never could have laid claim to complete originality. They are always fashioned after a model, in which the beginning artist believes his ideal to be realized, a model which he particularly loves, which he takes as a pattern, and which he attempts to equal. It was thus for J. Haydn, Mozart; and Beethoven, and will always be so, for it is natural. That which is or should be a priori original, invention and creation itself (not mere independence of form and exterior workmanship), takes time to express itself in its complete and true individuality, after it has liberated itself, more or less laboriously perfected, from everything foreign. All the more reason why we may not expect or desire independently formed, freely evident originality in every aspect of the present First Symphony by Mr Schumann. It suffices that a not insignificant ability to create idiomatically shines throughout, yea expresses itself unrestrained, so that one is justified in building not just small hopes in the presence of the usual technical merits.[33]

The review is essentially fair in observing Schumann's reliance on Schubert's style and also accurate in its recognition of Schumann's technical competence. The critic chooses some harsh phrases, perhaps, for a basically favourable notice, but this lends a sense of impartiality to the essay.

In a letter to Carl Koßmaly later that year Schumann expresses dismay at this review, though he closes with a hint that the critic was not entirely imperceptive: 'If you had heard the symphony, you would have let loose and cursed, I believe, at the review you read in the old music journal. The review was written by a well-known (otherwise not entirely dumb) sycophant of Mendelssohn's here, who [i.e. the sycophant] was

---

[32] A translation of the first part of this review appears at the beginning of ch. 1.
[33] '*Leipzig*. (Beschluss)', col. 331.

angered that I was first among the young artists to write a symphony that had an effect.'[34] Schumann obviously did not regard the *Lobgesang* Symphony, first performed at Leipzig in 1840, as falling in the same genre as a purely instrumental work; Mendelssohn's Third Symphony would not be heard until 1842, the remaining symphonies only after Mendelssohn's death. Schumann always honoured Mendelssohn as a composer, and Mendelssohn continued to the end of his life as a tireless advocate of Schumann's symphonies in Leipzig, but we cannot miss the sense of rivalry Schumann expresses in his reaction to the *AMZ* review. Gerald Abraham has made much of Mendelssohn's influence on Schumann in his later years,[35] and the notion seems generally true. But in the specific history of Op. 38 we see a more complicated relationship unfolding. Schumann did not reveal his piece to Mendelssohn until he had finished the orchestration and slightly revised it once; the conductor then served as technical adviser and agent for its successful performance. Though Schumann writes of Mendelssohn's 'corrections' to his score, as we have seen earlier, the sound of the piece suggests that the conductor had little direct influence on Schumann's style of orchestration, even though Mendelssohn must have been a great help in the composer's constant re-evaluation of the scoring.

Schumann gave his own estimate of the reception accorded the first performance of Op. 38 a month after the première in another letter to Carl Koßmaly, 'I wish you knew my symphony. The performance gave me—and others—such joy; for it was enthusiastically received, I believe, like no recent symphony since Beethoven's.'[36] If the composer conveniently forgot the reception of the Great C-major Symphony, he did not exaggerate much, none the less: no other première of a symphony apart from Schubert's had caused such a stir in Leipzig since the first performance of Beethoven's Ninth in 1826. Part of the sensation surrounding the Spring Symphony resulted from simple surprise about Schumann's 'newly' discovered talents, part from the composer's adaptation of the Schubertian manner to his own uses,

[34] Erler, *Briefe*, i. 269.

[35] Abraham makes his strongest statement on this point in *A Hundred Years of Music*, 4th edn. (London, 1974), 58; for all this, he finds Schumann a more interesting symphonist than Mendelssohn.

[36] Erler, *Briefe*, i. 258–9.

part from the careful preparation by Mendelssohn's orchestra, and part from the glamour of the occasion engendered by his wife's presence. Just as the sketches of the First Symphony reveal a certain amount of calculation, the events leading to the successful première show the methodical nature of Schumann's strategy, which he pursued with confidence because it had been employed profitably before in conjunction with the G-minor Symphony.

4 Publishing the Spring Symphony: The Second Version of Op. 38

Schumann had observed in connection with Schubert's Great C-major Symphony that a successful première at the Gewandhaus constituted a strong recommendation to Leipzig publishers, and the appearance of a ready purchaser for the Spring Symphony immediately after its first performance provides one more indication of the initial sensation it caused. Business dealings in this situation transpired informally at first—a word from an interested party in the concert hall to the composer. Schumann's buyers, the Härtels, had also purchased Schubert's symphony immediately after its triumphant Leipzig performance in 1839. The brothers occupied positions on the board of the Gewandhaus and regularly attended concerts, most probably including the benefit for the pension fund on 31 March 1841. Perhaps as the result of a verbal suggestion Schumann spent the days until 4 April 'polishing up the symphony',[1] and three days later he reached an oral agreement for its publication with the Härtels, sending written confirmation on 8 April.[2]

We would expect this transaction to close a stage in the textual history of Op. 38, but in fact it leads to a long series of further revisions. Schumann insisted on testing his instrumentation once more and did not deliver the autograph score or manuscript parts immediately to Breitkopf for engraving. While Schumann waited for yet another opportunity to hear his scoring, he made some major changes, and the extra performance yielded more adjustments.

The first possibility for another hearing came as the result of correspondence with Hyppolyte André Chélard, master of the court chapel at Weimar. He wrote to Clara on 22 March 1841 expressing curiosity about the rumoured première of Schumann's

---

[1] *Haushaltbücher*, p. 179.
[2] The date of sale, 7 April, can be found in the household accounts, ibid., and the record of correspondence comes from the *Briefverzeichnis*, p. 363, no. 755, 'das Geschäft wegen d.[er] Symphonie abzuschließen'.

symphony and to Robert on 29 May enquiring, 'Is there no way of having you both here for an official concert where one could hear your new symphony?'[3] Schumann replied on 6 June with reservations about a large public performance during the summer, partly because Clara was pregnant but also because he seems to have felt that his piece was not sufficiently polished:

We are busy and happy, and become ever more so. You could have been convinced of this from our concert. How I wish you might have been there on that evening at the Leipzig Gewandhaus—and how I should have liked you to hear my symphony. Would this perhaps be possible now? We have long intended a summer excursion, and would like to go by way of Weimar and Rudolfstadt, etc. How lovely it would be if we could present a small concert *among ourselves*—for it is not a good time for a public one now, and my wife does not appear to desire it particularly. I would also be glad to hear some of your compositions and you leading your orchestra. If this could be done, then we would go by way of Weimar and would spend a few days in your amiable vicinity. It would need to take place at the end of *July*, because my wife *may not* travel after that time.[4]

The Weimar concert could not be organized during the summer for lack of time and would wait until November. But Schumann did take up the Spring Symphony briefly in June to pursue a scheme for drawing just a bit more profit and renown from the piece. On 11 June he sent a letter to the King of Saxony, Friedrich August II, requesting permission for a dedication to the monarch, an act which would bring some sort of reward as well as favour in the capital city.[5] Friedrich was a particularly avid patron of the arts, and he had just recently agreed to subvene the creation of a conservatory in Leipzig at the behest of Mendelssohn.[6] Schumann's enquiry about the dedication prompted another review of the score on 12 June; he received the desired permission from the King's chamberlain in a letter dated 13 June.[7]

---

[3] Wolfgang Boetticher (ed.), *Briefe und Gedichte aus dem Album Robert und Clara Schumanns* (Leipzig, 1979), 42–3.

[4] Erler, *Briefe*, i. 261.

[5] *Haushaltbücher*, p. 185.

[6] Mendelssohn discussed the matter with Schumann and may have sought to enlist him at this point for the faculty; ibid. 184; n. 237, p. 711.

[7] Wolfgang Boetticher, 'Robert Schumann an Seine Königliche Majestät', *Die Musik*, xxxiii (1940), 61.

By mid-June 1841 Schumann had made some progress toward the publication of the symphony, but he still had not secured the crucial test performance. The composer writes with a guilty conscience to Härtel on 23 June:

> The symphony goes badly; it lies there ready—but I must hear it through again once, and at this time of year there is so little opportunity. The music festival [in Weimar?] of which I wrote has been postponed until September—and so in the end I would need to wait that long. In any case, however, I imagine that I will be able to send you the manuscript by September.[8]

In the period just following this communication to his publisher, Schumann took a vacation with Clara in the vicinity of Dresden and concerned himself with several other projects[9] before turning back to Op. 38. In the mean time, Hermann Härtel suggested that the composer hire the Gewandhaus for a rehearsal of the symphony instead of waiting until the autumn for a public performance. This prompted Schumann to give his revisions of Op. 38 over to be copied into what was probably a new score, recording payment of seven thalers to a 'copyist for symphony' on 27 July.[10] On 2 August Schumann turned to the acting conductor of the Gewandhaus, Ferdinand David, with Härtel's plan. The violinist describes the meeting in a humorous letter to Mendelssohn, taking special note of the composer's usual reticence in personal dealings:

> Yesterday Schumann was at my house and remained before me in silence for an hour, out of which it finally became clear to me that he would like to hear his symphony in public once again. I suggested to him to do it at a horn sectional, whereupon he gave it to be understood through signs that he wanted to pay for a rehearsal in order to go through it thoroughly. Then he smoked two cigars, placed his hand twice over his mouth because a syllable wanted to escape, took his hat, forgot his gloves, nodded his head, went to the wrong door, then to the right one, and he was gone.[11]

---

[8] Jansen, *Briefe*, p. 431.

[9] *Haushaltbücher*, pp. 185–6; also n. 243, p. 711.

[10] Ibid. 189. The reference 'for symphony' must allude to Op. 38, the only piece ready for and in need of copying at this point; and Schumann could not refer to parts here, for his letter to Raimund Härtel on 3 August strongly suggests that the parts had not yet been produced and would cost substantially more (9 thalers).

[11] Julius Eckhardt, *Ferdinand David und die Familie Mendelssohn-Bartholdy*, (Leipzig, 1888), 130–1.

Schumann sent the details of the plan to Raimund Härtel the following day, excusing his tardiness with a mild prevarication:

> After a long illness which prevented me from all strenuous work, I have come far enough with the symphony to have it performed within eight days. I return to the friendly suggestion of your brother 'to arrange a special rehearsal at the Gewandhaus and to discuss the expenses with each other'. If you wish, we will divide them. The rehearsal will cost about twenty thalers, the copying [of the parts] about nine thalers.—These last you will use directly for the engraving, which will begin immediately then, so that the symphony could go out into the world at the beginning of October. Kindly write to me whether this is all right, in order that I might discuss it further with David. . . .[12]

The approaching rehearsal provided the occasion for yet another review ending on 8 August, consultation with David on 10 August, and completion of the corrected parts the next day. On 12 August David wrote to Schumann, 'The only time for your rehearsal is tomorrow, Friday, at 10 o'clock. . . . If you are satisfied with tomorrow morning, then, tell the bearer of this [message], who will make all the arrangements immediately.'[13] After this rendition on 13 August (the 'fantasy' for piano and orchestra, later transformed into the first movement of his Piano Concerto, Op. 54, was also performed) the composer further revised the parts and sent them to his publisher on 16 August.[14]

The first edition of the Spring Symphony consisted of parts without a printed score, a fairly common practice in the publication of orchestral music during this period. German orchestras were usually small, and they were often led by the first violinist whose part, along with the others, was supplied richly with cues. Reading proof of an orchestral piece printed in this fashion consumed a good deal of time; in addition Schumann wished to be particulary meticulous in his first symphonic print. He corrected the text for the first edition in three separate stages, one beginning on 6 September and lasting

[12] Jansen, *Briefe*, p. 432.

[13] Werner · Schwarz, 'Eine Musikerfreundschaft des 19. Jahrhunderts', *Zum 70. Geburtstag von Joseph Müller-Blattau*, ed. Christoph Helmut Mahling (Kassel, 1960), 285–6.

[14] *Haushaltbücher*, p. 191.

until 29 September, a second from 8 October until 12 October, and the last from 18 October to 20 October. An unpublished letter on 19 October to André Chélard concerning arrangements for the postponed Weimar concert reveals that Schumann corrected the printed parts by comparing them with a manuscript score:

> Not until today, my honoured friend, could I reply to you. A few clouds towered up against our Weimar excursion but have passed away in the mean time. *We will come, then.* My wife wants to play the Capriccio in A with orchestra by Mendelssohn and then four solo pieces. Is that all right with you? I cannot part at the moment with the score of my symphony, because I need it for revision of the proof. You will receive it in eight days. The day of the dress rehearsal will probably be the 20th of November? Then we will arrive the day before. Kindly write to us something more definite about it![15]

Chélard was probably the first to purchase the printed parts,[16] which appeared on 10 November 1841 to Schumann's exclamation of 'joy' in the household accounts.[17] The composer had already been paid his honorarium of 120 thalers on 26 September (see Table 9 below for a summary of the chronology),[18] and this was later supplemented in December 1841 by the gift of a golden snuffbox from the King of Saxony for the dedication of the piece.[19]

Many of the documents relating to the chronology for the first edition of Op. 38 are unfortunately lost to us. We do not

---

[15] The German text reads: 'Erst heute, mein verehrter Freund, kann ich Ihnen antworten. Es hatten sich gegen unserem Weimar Ausflug einige Wolken aufgethürmt, aber indeß jetzt wieder vergangen. *Wir kommon also.* Meine Frau will das Capriccio von Mendelssohn in A mit Orchester und dann vier Solostücke spielen. Ist Ihnen das Recht? Die Partitur meiner Symphonie kann ich im Augenblick noch nicht mißen, da ich die zur Revision der Correctur brauche. Sie erhalten sie in 8 Tagen. Der Tag der Hauptprobe ist wohl den 20sten November? Dann kommen wir Tags vorher an. Schreiben Sie uns darüber gefälligst was bestimmteres!' This letter can be found in the Musikabteilung of the Staatsbibliothek Preußischer Kulturbesitz, Berlin, Mus. ep. Schumann 13; my thanks to Dr Rudolf Elvers for permission to quote it here. Schumann's first reply to Chélard's proposal for a fall concert can be seen in Erler, *Briefe*, i. 267–8.

[16] Ibid. 271.

[17] *Haushaltbücher*, p. 199.

[18] Ibid. 671.

[19] Boetticher, 'Seine Königliche Majestät', p. 61. Boetticher gives the date of the royal chamberlain's letter incorrectly as 31 October 1841, but Nauhaus corrects this to 31 December 1841; Schumann lists receipt on 3 January 1841, *Haushaltbücher*, p. 204; n. 290, p. 717.

TABLE 9.   *Chronology of the first edition of Op. 38*

Date	Activity	Source
4 Apr.	Completes polishing the score	*Haushaltbücher*
7 Apr.	Sale of symphony to Härtel	*Haushaltbücher*
8 Apr.	Letter confirming sale	*Briefverzeichnis*
29 May	Letter from Chélard about performance	*Album*
6 June	Schumann requests July performance	Erler
12 June	Revision of Op. 38	*Haushaltbücher*
23 June	Letter to Härtel promising September delivery	Jansen
27 July	Payment 'to copyist for symphony'	*Haushaltbücher*
2 Aug.	Visit to David about special rehearsal	*Haushaltbücher*
3 Aug.	Letter to Härtel about special rehearsal	Jansen
8 Aug.	Review of Op. 38 completed	*Haushaltbücher*
10 Aug.	Review of Op. 38 with David	*Haushaltbücher*
11 Aug.	Correction of parts completed	*Haushaltbücher*
13 Aug.	Rehearsal of Op. 38 in Gewandhaus	*Haushaltbücher*
14–15 Aug.	Revision of parts	*Haushaltbücher*
16 Aug.	Parts delivered to Härtel	*Haushaltbücher*
6–29 Sept.	First proof of printed edition	*Haushaltbücher*
26 Sept.	Receipt of 120 thalers honorarium	*Haushaltbücher*
8–12 Oct.	Second proof of printed edition	*Haushaltbücher*
18–20 Oct.	Third proof of printed edition	*Haushaltbücher*
10 Nov.	Publication of First Symphony	*Haushaltbücher*

know the location of the rehearsal parts that served as exemplars for the engraver of the first edition, if indeed Breitkopf or Schumann saw fit to preserve them at all. And the manuscript full score for which the composer paid on 27 July and which he mentions to Chélard on 19 October has also disappeared.[20] We can imagine how Schumann's second manuscript of Op. 38 might have looked based on other orchestral scores of this kind made for the composer. A copyist would have entered much of the music, but substantially revised passages would feature some lines written by the composer (usually the melody and the bass)

[20] The autograph differs so extensively from the print that it could not have been used either in August for conducting or in September for correcting parts, and other manuscripts of the symphony prove unlikely candidates for various reasons. Roughly contemporary manuscripts of the score include British Library Add. 31803 and Library of Congress ML 31.H43a N. 89 used to engrave the second edition of the symphony; the relationship of these two scores to the compositional history of the symphony appears in ch. 5.

with the remaining staves completed by the scrivener.[21] Lacking the parts used by the engraver or the hypothetical manuscript score, we can only compare the autograph score with the printed parts of the first edition[22] and treat Schumann's changes after the individual performances on 31 March and 13 August as one unit of cumulative revision.

The quality of the first edition is only fair, in spite of Schumann's lengthy bouts of correction. The parts contain typographical errors, such as an unmarked first ending for the first movement in the first flute part, the omission of a measure from the second clarinet part in the first trio (Breitkopf stamped this correction into some copies), a miscounting of rests in the triangle part for the first movement, causing an entrance four measures late in the development section, and a misprint of the measures 5 and 6 of the first movement in the third and fourth horns. The parts also present no consistency in articulation: for example, the main theme in the first movement features staccatos for the woodwinds but not for the first and second violins playing the same melody. The 1841 edition does provide a sufficiently sound text, however, to permit an accurate assessment of the changes Schumann made to the musical syntax and scoring of Op. 38 after two more hearings.

REVISIONS IN THE MUSICAL SYNTAX FOR THE FIRST EDITION

Even after the première on 31 March Schumann made relatively major alterations to the Spring Symphony, changing the place-

[21] Just such practices occur prominently in the autograph of the D-minor Symphony in the Gesellschaft der Musikfreunde, A-292, and in the autograph of the C-major Symphony, Österreichische Nationalbibliothek, PhA 1281. See discussions of these manuscripts in my 'Robert Schumann: The Creation of the Symphonic Works' (PhD dissertation, University of Chicago, 1980), 205–6 and 281–8.

[22] The title page on the first violin part reads: SYMPHONIE / für grosses Orchester / componirt / und / Sr. Majestät dem Könige von Sachsen / FRIEDRICH AUGUST / in tiefster Ehrfurcht zugeeignet / von / ROBERT SCHUMANN / Op. 38—Pr. 6 Thlr. 15 Ngr. / Eigentum der Verleger / Leipzig bei Breitkopf & Härtel / 6595 / Eingetragen in das Vereins-Archiv. Copies of these parts are located at the Gesellschaft der Musikfreunde, Vienna, under the siglum XIII 21539, at the Österreichische National-bibliothek under the call number BA 368, and in the collection of Kurt Hofmann (see his *Die Erstdrucke der Werke von Robert Schumann* (Tutzing, 1979), 89, 416). For this study I have relied on the parts found in the Gesellschaft.

ment of certain musical gestures, reharmonizing one passage,
and rearranging some metrical relationships. His reconsideration
of musical gesture falls in the final movement, where he returns
to the problematic placement of the flute cadenza and the main
theme which develops from it. He decides that the cadenza
seems most appropriate as part of the retransition. It had appeared
in the March version leading into the exposition, but the
composer deletes this occurrence and with it the repeat of the
first phrase in the main theme. In a parallel alteration, he also
abridges a similar passage for the violins in the first ending to
the exposition (Ex. 4.1a), replacing it with a much more concise
return (Ex. 4.1b). Having diminished or deleted these two effusive

Example 4.1a   Schumann, Op. 38, mvt. 4, first ending in autograph

Example 4.1*b*   Schumann, Op. 38, mvt. 4, first ending in 1841 print

gestures in the exposition, Schumann feels he may indulge himself in the retransition. He removes the extensive trills found in the manuscript score (an idea listed in the original sketches as a 'variant' on 11ᵛ), and he replaces them with a series of bucolic horn calls in the printed version (mm. 170–1), followed by the flute cadenza (mm. 172–3) which leads directly into the first phrase of the theme (mm. 174–7). The violins then repeat this first phrase (mm. 178–81) before continuing. The main theme in the recapitulation now appears to grow out of the flute cadenza. We should recall that both of these changes concern passages that Schumann had altered during the orchestration of the first version. The flute cadenza at the retransition as well as the arrangement of phrasing for the main theme in exposition and recapitulation both recall the original conception in the sketches.

The printed edition also displays Schumann's return to his first conception of the opening horn and trumpet fanfare. I suggested earlier that he had already changed the opening pitch from B flat to the D found in the first layer of sketches during the first rehearsal of the piece (see above p. 87), but the revision does not appear in his autograph score. Schumann must have had his copyist enter the alteration in the conducting score mentioned on 27 July, from which the parts for the rehearsal on 13 August were taken and used afterwards by the engraver of the printed edition.

The most remarkable revision of pitch in the printed edition comes understandably in the coda for the first movement, which had already undergone some extensive reworking before the performance on 31 March. The closing section as it first appears in the March version consists of paired phrases linked by bridges (see above ch. 3, Table 8). The first pair involves an exact repetition of a unit developed by linking fragments of the main theme with a motive from the second transition, ending in a lengthy group of cadential figures (45^r–49^v). For the printed version Schumann first removes the motivic material from the second transition, continuing instead to develop motives from the main theme by fragmenting the original four-measure units into two-measure units (mm. 397–404 and 421–8, see Table 10). The result is more coherent and also better emphasizes the large-scale rhythmic acceleration in this passage from longer sequences to shorter sequences using the same material.

Logic of progression also governs the composer's re-harmonization of measures 397–404. In the autograph, measures

TABLE 10. *Revisions in Mvt. I Coda for the First Edition of Op. 38*

Location		Material		Harmonization (B^b major)	
Autograph	Print	Autograph	Print	Autograph	Print
46^v–47^r	397–98*	2nd transition	Mth	$V^{6/5}/II$–II	$V^{6/5}/II$–II
	399–400			$V^{6/5}/N$–N	$V^{6/5}$–I
	401–402			iv^6–$iv^{6/+3}$†	$ii^{6/5}$–vii^{o7}/V
	missing			$vii^{o4/2}$–Ger^{+6}	
	403–404			$I^{6/4}$–$i^{6/4}$–V^7	$I^{6/4}$–$i^{6/4}$–V^7
48^v–49^v	421–422	2nd transition	Mth	$V^{6/5}/II$–II	$V^{6/5}/II$–II
	423–424			$V^{6/5}/N$–N	$V^{6/5}N$–N
	425–426			iv^6–$iv^{6/+3}$	iv^6–$iv^{6/+3}$
	427–428			$vii^{o4/2}$–Ger^{+6}	$vii^{o4/2}$–Ger^{+6}
	429			$I^{6/4}$	$I^{6/4}$

* Numbers do not reflect anticipation of one eight-note in each measure.

† An augmented sub-dominant chord with minor third is the enharmonic equivalent of a Neapolitan chord.

397–404 and 421–8 feature the same harmonic scheme. In the printed version Schumann shortens the first phrase of the pair, employing a more usual root movement in measures 397 to 404, while retaining the exotic assemblage of Neapolitan and augmented-sixth chords for the parallel passage in measures 412–28 (see Table 10). The movement from the more customary to the more exotic helps to shape the passage overall and intensifies the sense of pressing forward, just as the motivic revisions had. And in turn the increased acceleration and direction creates even more contrast with the lyrical interlude that follows. These two substantial revisions in the first movement's coda give more support to the notion that Schumann did not sketch it in detail before writing the March version. The long series of alterations found in that manuscript and in subsequent versions display the kinds of problems that ordinarily would have been resolved during the creation of a continuity draft.

The most fascinating changes in the musical syntax of the score concern problems of mensuration, for they reveal the extent to which Schumann involved himself in the practical exigencies of performance. The revision in the time signature and barring of the second movement is actually indicated in the LC autograph though left unrealized until the appearance of the printed version. Schumann had vacillated in his sketch about the proper metre for the slow movement, suggesting first 6/8 then 6/4 time (8^r). In the autograph he scores the movement in 6/8 time, marking it 'Adagio molto', but adds a note later specifying a barring 'in 3/8' ('Nach 3/8tel zu setzen'). At the same time he alters the tempo designation to 'Larghetto' (59^r), and this solution appears in the print. During one of his visits with Mendelssohn, perhaps, or at one of the many rehearsals, the composer decided that the compound metre created too much ambiguity about the value of the beat. He indicates the eighth note as the basic pulse in this movement by casting it in 3/8 and giving a metronome marking to the eighth note of 66 beats per minute. The last movement undergoes a related though less extensive change from common time to an *alla breve* signature, with the pulse assigned to the half note at 116 beats per minute. Here the new mensuration together with the metronome marking gives the impression of a tempo faster than the original sign might suggest and avoids any confusion left by the somewhat

complicated combination of 'allegro animato e grazioso'. The appearance of metronome markings in the rest of the print indicates the composer's concern with transmitting his ideas precisely to the conductor or leader.

The same desire for metric precision motivates a set of changes for the retransition in the first movement. In Schumann's sketches this passage returns to the heraldic beginning of the slow introduction with its attendant mensuration in common time (6^r). When he reached the autograph, the composer cast his quotation of the fanfare motto in 2/4 time over a dominant pedal (autograph, 38^v–40^r), but the answering phrase (40^r) remained in common time with a sudden ritard to a maestoso tempo. In the printed version, however, Schumann rewrites the answering phrase in augmented values, keeping the same time signature (mm. 309–16). In this way the desired ritard occurs automatically, eliminating any difficulty the conductor and ensemble might have in the sudden change of tempo. A similar case occurs in Schumann's alteration of note values for the coda of the first movement. The composer had already thought to rebar the last cadential section of this coda, changing the mensuration to 'alla breve' in the autograph (53^r–56^r, see above, p. 73). For the print he rewrites this entire passage (mm. 483–515) in notes diminished by one half, retaining the 2/4 signature and rendering the desired change of speed involuntary. Such revisions may have come about as the result of Mendelssohn's, David's, or players' suggestions during rehearsals. Schumann's experiments with the symphony benefited from the peculiar familial nature (Schumann's own characterization in his reviews) of the Gewandhaus orchestra and the composer's close relationship with its members.

If we regard the revisions found in the musical syntax of the printed version of Op. 38 as a whole, we see that Schumann was still involved at a late juncture in the kinds of compositional decisions made by most composers of instrumental music during the initial sketching or during the translation of the sketch into score. I do not view this last statement as pejorative: Schumann engaged in this leisurely practice because the circumstances in Leipzig afforded him an indulgent conductor and orchestra of the first rank as well as ready access to publishers over whom he had some influence as editor of a critical review. The nature

of Schumann's compositional process in the later stages of
Op. 38 results in large measure from empirical proclivities which
he fortunately had the means to follow.

REVISIONS IN THE SCORING FOR THE FIRST EDITION

By far the majority of Schumann's revisions for his first printed
edition of Op. 38 concern orchestration, and they are too
numerous to recount here in full. The principles behind Schumann's alterations are relatively simple, however, and can be
demonstrated by just a few examples. The print shows many
passages where Schumann became convinced that he had
overscored the 31 March performance, resulting in the deletion
of many tied chordal accompaniments found in the autograph.
The chords often appear in the winds supporting melodies in
the strings. A good example can be found in the passage just
preceding the first movement's retransition. In the scoring for
the autograph (Ex. 4.2a) the violins present the melody, answered
later by the woodwinds. The non-melodic voices accompany
with chords generally held for at least a full measure, producing
a relatively opaque texture. For the printed edition (Ex. 4.2b)
most of the parts retain their pitches, but the composer replaces
some of the held chords in the trumpets, timpany, and upper
trombones with eighth-note punctuations, while positioning the
bass trombone in the same octave as the cellos and bassoons. An
analogous example can be found at the end of the first movement
('Animato' 85^r ff., mm. 381 ff.), where the many tied half-note
chords in the flute and oboe have been removed largely in
favour of eighth-note punctuations, while sustained harmonic
support appears gradually, first in the bassoons and then in the
clarinets. In most of these passages Schumann places the melody
in only one voice (often in the violins), and he reduces the
texture in the print to help the melodic line penetrate its
accompaniment.

On some occasions the composer clarifies the texture by
rescoring the melody for additional parts or changing melodic
articulation. In the much revised violin line at the beginning of
the first movement's main theme (see Exx. 3.6a and 3.6b above)

Example 4.2*a* Schumann, Op. 38, mvt. 1, development immediately preceding retransition in autograph

Example 4.2*b*   Schumann, Op. 38, mvt. 1, development immediately preceding retransition in 1841 print

Schumann adopts a new doubling for the print, adding the first violins to the flutes, rather than confining the first violins solely to the punctuating chords found in the March version. Schumann also alters string rearticulations on some occasions, as in the coda to the finale where he replaces the sixteenth notes of the autograph score (105^r ff.) with more forceful eighth-note rearticulations in the print (mm. 301 ff.). This change re-emphasizes the violin counterpoint in the midst of a busy texture.

The two combined means of adjusting balance in the printed version of Op. 38 merely follow the course Schumann had charted earlier during his revision of the autograph. For a given passage we can sometimes trace a progressive set of changes, like those for the coda to the third movement. In the previous chapter we saw Schumann's initial scoring for this passage: an extremely heavy accompaniment supported a relatively weak melody in the woodwinds (Ex. 3.5a). Schumann adjusted the balance by relieving the chordal texture with rests and reinforcing both the melody in the flutes and its counterpoint in the first bassoon with doublings respectively by the first violins and cellos (Ex. 3.5b). The printed version of the coda (Ex. 4.3) displays the continuation of the process: the second violins play the melody with the firsts and flutes, the violas have assumed the chords formerly played by the seconds, and the incessant timpani pedal falls away together with the trumpet punctuations. Over the course of three successive revisions following a consistent line of thought, Schumann has gradually brought his melody out of the shadows by painting it in lighter hues while stripping away some of the dark colours in the background.

One of the most striking examples of Schumann's progressive refinement in balance can be found at the beginning of the second movement. In his ultimate autograph version of the main theme the composer had arrived at a simplified texture with the melody in the lower range of the first violins in unison, a pattern of moving thirty-second notes in the second violins, and subtle syncopations in the violas (already a reduction in activity compared with the first scoring, see above Ex. 3.3 and 3.4). In the printed edition Schumann continues the process by further reducing both the second violins and violas to syncopated motion primarily in eighth-note rhythms (the sixteenth notes are tied; see Ex. 4.4) and by removing all of the arpeggiated thirty-second

Example 4.3   Schumann, Op. 38, mvt. 3, coda in 1841 print

Example 4.4   Schumann, Op. 38, mvt. 2, string parts for beginning of main theme in 1841 print

notes overloading the texture. The lessened activity in the accompaniment entails a complementary accentuation of the melody by returning half of the first violins to the upper octave. In making this final revision to the scoring of the second movement's main theme, Schumann has come full circle to his initial conception. The original pencilled layer of his draft (see Ex. 2.8 above) suggests a melody scored for the first violins in their upper, more audible octave with supporting eighth notes for the violas (the composer specifies '*divisi*' for the first violins and '*32stele*' for the violas only later in ink as he transfers the passage to score); accompanimental figuration predominantly in sixteenth notes appears for the bridge to the first variation and thirty-second notes do not appear until the bridge to the second variation. Schumann's experimentation with the score only led him back to the sound he had originally heard in his mind.

Another complementary alteration of the balance between melody and accompaniment can be found under quite different circumstances in the finale at the end of the main theme (f. 85 in the autograph, mm. 31–41 of the print). In the March version the composer writes a series of cadential figures beginning in the strings and answered by the woodwinds, with the first oboe and both clarinets playing a melodic line ornamented by the flutes and bassoons, while the timpany, trumpets, and horns reinforce the rhythm of the figure (Ex. 4.5a). Schumann concludes that the melodic line does not articulate distinctly in the woodwind answer, for he re-orchestrates this passage in the printed version, giving the initial figure to the lower strings and the reply to the first and second violins (Ex. 4.5b). This latter antiphonal division of the melody takes advantage of the seating arrangement at the Gewandhaus, where the first and second violins occupied opposite sides at the front of the stage.[23] It also marks a return to the sketches (10^r), where the violins alone carry the melodic line. The composer confines the brass to occasional punctuations and assigns the woodwinds chordal accompaniments, deleting the sixteenth-note embellishments entirely from the flutes and bassoons. The harsh dissonance of B flat against A, continually reiterated by the strings in the sketch and the March version, has been limited in the print to occasional interjections spaced at a vertical distance to ameliorate the clash. Schumann has subordinated musical syntax to sonority in this instrumentation: he removes the ornamentation and mutes the dissonance merely to clarify texture. The passage summarizes Schumann's transformation of the heavily scored March version into the more transparent printed version.

Schumann's continual return in his printed version to scorings intimated in his original sketches suggests that his fundamental concept of symphonic sound remains constant; he merely lacks assurance about the best method by which to realize his initial aural image. He had acquired substantial experience with scoring before he sketched the Spring Symphony and knew the kind of orchestral sound he preferred, but his acquaintance with the technique of orchestration had grown distant. The numerous changes within the autograph itself and between the autograph and printed versions show Schumann's lack of practice, but nowhere does the composer drastically alter the range in which he uses an instrument, nor his preferences for certain combinations of colour, that is to say, his basic notion of orchestral sound. He uses the repeated live performances of the symphony before publication to bolster his confidence in his original conception. The print presents an adjusted and polished version of Op. 38, more complete in its articulation and dynamic markings, prag-

[23] Daniel J. Koury, *Orchestral Performance Practices in the Nineteenth Century: Size, Proportions and Seating* (Ann Arbor, 1986), 207.

matically refined in its texture, and therefore better fitted to produce the desired result. Because Schumann viewed Op. 38 as the foundation of his reputation, he carefully adapted the symphony for the kind of ensemble he expected to perform it.

REVIEW OF THE FIRST PRINTED VERSION

The appearance of the first printed edition of Op. 38 on 10 November 1841 placed Schumann on the brink of recognition as a major composer. He would need some good press for publicity, and he could not use his own journal without injuring his credibility as an independent critic. He relied therefore on the *Allgemeine Musikalische Zeitung*, Breitkopf and Härtel's house organ, to provide the only substantial review, and he apparently had no qualms about this particular conflict of interest. The reviewer, August Kahlert, provides a commonplace account in many respects. He devotes a good deal of space at the beginning of the article to the composer's past accomplishments as journalist and his propensity to write solely for the piano, following a form established by the first reviews of the première. He mentions just briefly the programmatic concept behind the piece and gives what seems to be in *AMZ* reviews an obligatory inventory of the various themes. Kahlert's most interesting comments concern Schumann's orchestration, for he claims at the beginning of his essay that Schumann had always written for keyboard with orchestral effects in mind, and he goes on to observe:

The instrumentation presents much that is surprising and unusual, often truly beautiful in its effect. On the whole it follows that which has been customary since Weber, without disregarding its extension by Meyerbeer. The employment of deep oboe notes in Weber, which overstep the range of the clarinet, the application of the horns, of the violoncellos, are elements which the new school will no longer gladly forgo. They yield the means of creating that romantic chiaroscuro in which individually aimed lights stand out all the more vividly, through which a kind of coloration arises which was not common in Mozart. Raphael's homogeneous harmonization of colour is different from the romantic illumination in Correggio or in Rembrandt. This comparison provides a criterion for recent instrumentation. Schumann has employed

Example 4.5a   Schumann, Op. 38, mvt. 4, end of main theme in autograph

Example 4.5*b*   Schumann, Op. 38. mvt. 4, end of main theme in 1841 print

these means even to wrap the outlines of his melodies in an almost magical illumination. Here, at times, Franz Schubert's symphony also occurred to us.[24]

Schumann had mixed emotions about this assessment, writing to the critic on 10 May 1842, 'Thanks for the symphony review. An entirely polished performance would cast much in another light, I believe. The artist must be happy, however, if he arouses any sympathy at all in the critic—and I have done so in you, as every line of your essay testifies.'[25] Despite the composer's objections, Kahlert had viewed the scoring shrewdly, both its similarities to Schubert's writing and Schumann's attempt— evident throughout his many revisions—to highlight his melodies against a basically dark background.

At the very close of his article Kahlert reminded Schumann that his work on the symphony had not been entirely completed: he called for a four-hand piano reduction of Op. 38, ostensibly to bring the symphony to the attention of an even wider audience. By the time Kahlert had published this suggestion in March 1842, Schumann had already reached the conclusion that his Spring Symphony would require promotion beyond the mere availability of printed parts and the publicity afforded by favourable reviews. In the course of pursuing this last pragmatic goal for the reception of Op. 38, he found that the text had not been completed entirely to his satisfaction, a discovery which opened a new chapter in the genesis of Op. 38.

[24] August Kahlert, '*Robert Schumann*: Symphonie für grosses Orchester, componirt von —. Op. 38. Leipzig, bei Breitkopf & Härtel. Preis 6 Thlr. 15 Ngr.', *AMZ*, xliv (1842), col. 270.

[25] Erler, *Briefe*, i. 278.

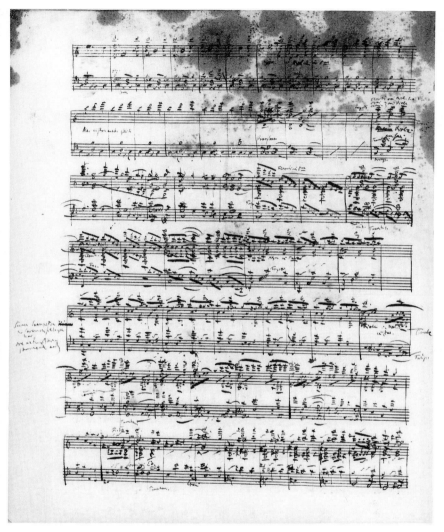

I Excerpt from Schumann's piano reduction of Beethoven's Leonore
Overture No. 3 (Bonn, Universitätsbibliothek, Schumann 16)

II Sketch of Op. 38, mvt. I to the middle of the main theme (Library of Congress, ML 96.S415 Case, 4ʳ)

III Sketch for Op. 38, mvt. I, end of main theme to second transition
(Library of Congress, ML 96.S415 Case, 4ᵛ)

IV Sketch for Op. 38, mvt. I, closing material and beginning of development (Library of Congress, ML 96.S415 Case, 5ʳ)

V Sketch for Op. 38, mvt. I, indicating repetition of main theme in D
(Library of Congress, ML 96.S415 Case, 5ᵛ)

VI Sketch for Op. 38, mvt. I, end of development, retransition, and
recapitulation of second theme (Library of Congress, ML 96.S415 Case, 6ʳ)

VII Sketch for Op. 38, mvt. I, end of continuity draft (Library of Congress, ML 96.S415 Case, 6ᵛ)

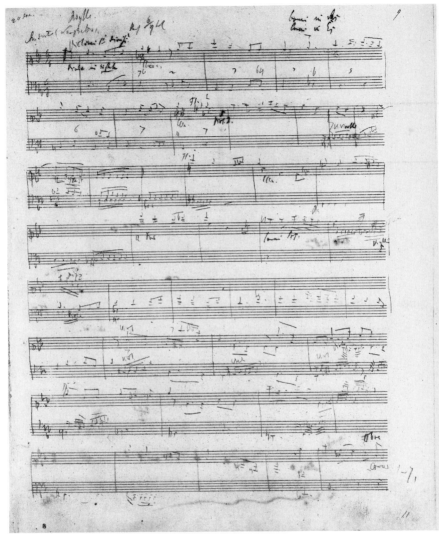

VIII Sketch of Op. 38, mvt. II (Library of Congress, ML 96.S415 Case, 8ʳ)

IX Sketch of Op. 38, bridge between mvts. II and III, Scherzo, and
beginning of trio I (Library of Congress, ML 96.S415 Case, 8ᵛ)

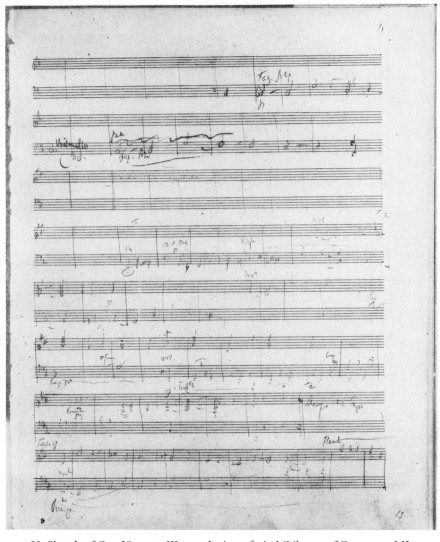

X   Sketch of Op. 38, mvt. III, conclusion of trio I (Library of Congress, ML 96.S415 Case, 9ʳ)

XI Sketch of Op. 38, coda to mvt. III and beginning of mvt. IV (Library of Congress, ML 96.S415 Case, 9ᵛ)

XII Sketch for Op. 38, mvt. IV, end of main theme and transition (Library of Congress, ML 96.S415 Case, 10^r)

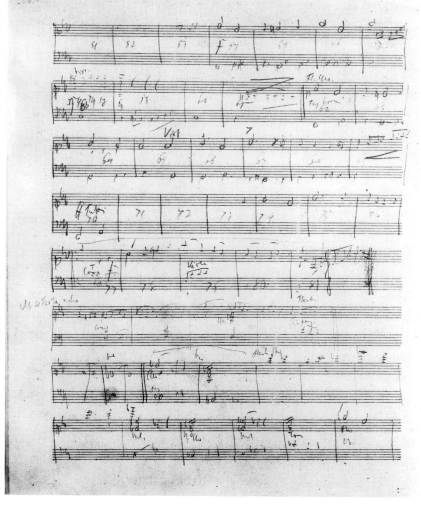

XIII Sketch for Op. 38, mvt. IV, second theme, closing, and beginning of development (Library of Congress, ML 96.S415 Case, 10ᵛ)

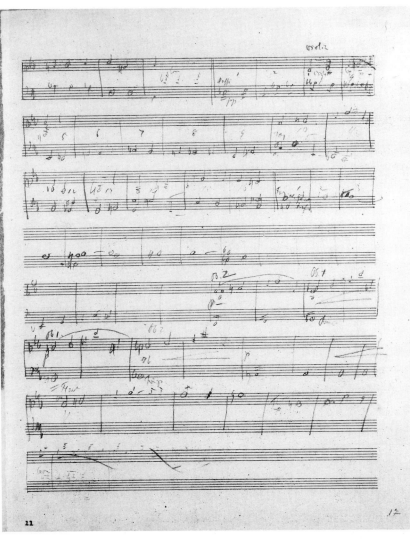

XIV Sketch for Op. 38, mvt. IV, model I, sequence and fragmentation
(Library of Congress, ML 96.S415 Case, 11ʳ)

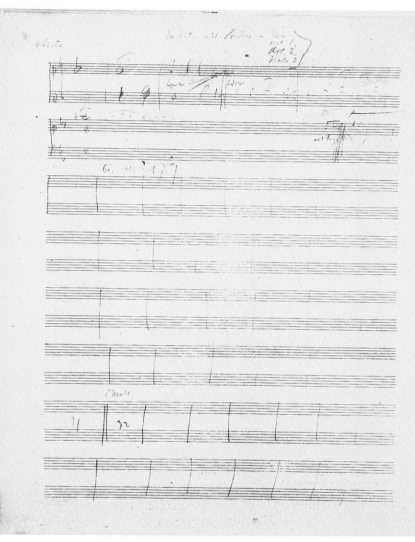

XV Sketch for Op. 38, mvt. IV, retransition, cadenza, and beginning of recapitulation (Library of Congress, ML 96.S415 Case, 11ᵛ)

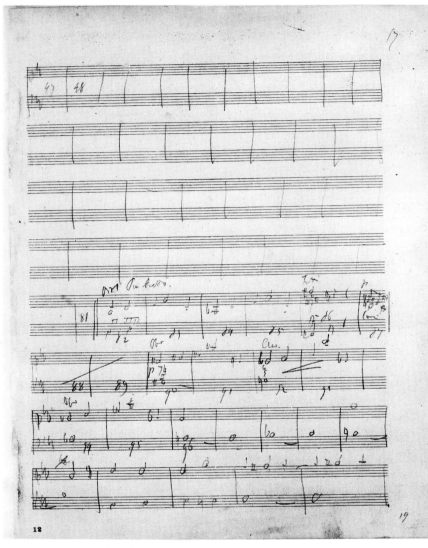

XVI Sketch for Op. 38, mvt. IV, end of recapitulation and beginning of coda (Library of Congress, ML 96.S415 Case, 12ʳ)

5 Promoting and Refining Op. 38: The Production of the Second Edition

Schumann's persistent concern for the fate of the Spring Symphony after the appearance of the printed parts in November of 1841 can be seen graphically on the first folio of his autograph, where he patiently recorded every known rendition of the piece from its première until 1852 (see Table 11). Schumann arranged some of the 43 performances himself and conducted several more, relying as he had previously on his wide circle of professional acquaintance and on Clara's fame as a pianist to secure a place for the work on concert programmes'. Each performance he heard or directed provided another opportunity to polish the score, and for concerts he could not attend he often provided written advice to the conductor on points of execution. At the end of this period he supervised publication of the piece in full score, incorporating in the text all the refinements gathered from ten years of listening and conducting.

Two public renditions of Op. 38 followed immediately on the appearance of the printed parts, the first in Leipzig at the Euterpe Music Club under the direction of Johann Verhulst and the other, after the summer's postponement, in Weimar under the direction of Chélard. Because the Euterpe and Gewandhaus shared many players already familiar with the piece, the composer probably did not need to say much to Verhulst about the details of the performance, though he attended both rehearsal and concert.[1] For the performance in Weimar Schumann sent written advice to Chélard: 'Most of the difficulty has been caused by the *Poco a poco accelerando* during the transition to the Allegro of the first movement, and then by the *1st Trio of the Scherzo*, and by the *close of the Scherzo* (Quasi presto). For these places I ask your particular attention and patience.' Schumann also pointed out two mistakes in the second clarinet's part, an incorrect rhythm in the second ending of the first movement

---

[1] *Haushaltbücher*, p. 199; see also Dz., 'Zweites Concert der Euterpe, den 15. Novbr.', *NZfM*, xv (1841), 172.

TABLE 11   *Performances of Op. 38 recorded by Schumann in the LC autograph*

City	Date	Performer
Leipzig	31.3.41	Mendelssohn, [Felix]
Leipzig	15.11.41	Verhulst, [Johann]
Weimar	21.11.41	Chélard, [André]
Rudolfstadt	21.1.42	Müller, [Friedrich]
Bremen	23.2.42	Riem, [Friedrich]
Bremen	4.11.42	Riem
Hamburg	5.3.42	Grund, [Friedrich]
Dresden	Winter 42	Hartung, [Johann]
Breslau	Winter 42	[not given]
Leipzig	3.11.42	David, [Ferdinand]
Oldenburg	4.42	Pott, [August]
Frankfurt	1.43	Guhr, [Karl]
Kassel	1.43	Spohr, [Ludwig]
Detmold	12.42	Kiel, [August]
Düsseldorf	4.44	Rietz, [Julius]
Berlin	2.43	Taubert, [Wilhelm]
Frankfurt	11.43	Guhr
Königsberg	Winter 43–44	Sobolewski, [Friedrich]
St Petersburg	Winter 44	[Schumann]
Leipzig	11.44	Gade, [Niels]
Leipzig	10.45	Mendelssohn
Dresden	8.45	[not given]
Halle	1.46	Franz, [Robert]
Rotterdam	1.46	[not given]
Utrecht	[1.46?]	[not given]
Copenhagen	1.46	Gläser, [Franz]
Vienna	1.1.47	[Schumann]
Leipzig	2.48	Gade
Dresden	2.48	Kunze, [Heinrich]
Prague	2.48	Caecilien Verein
Leipzig	12.48	Netzer, [Josef]
Utrecht	1.49	[not given]
Leipzig	7.10.49	Rietz
Magdeburg	10.49	Mühling, [Julius]
Leipzig	12.12.49	Riccius, [Karl]
Rotterdam	3.50	Dupont, [Johannes]
Frankfurt	3.1.51	Messer, [Franz]
Leipzig	1.51	Rietz

TABLE 11 *continued*

City	Date	Performer
Chemnitz	Winter 50–51	[not given]
Leipzig	3.51	Riccius
Basel	3.51	Reiter, [Ernst]
Düsseldorf	5.52	[Schumann]
Coblenz	Winter 51–52	Levy, [Joseph]

and the omission of a measure in the first trio of the third movement.[2] But at this juncture the composer did not express any dissatisfaction with his scoring, nor did he propose any minor changes to improve balance.

Schumann's endeavours to disseminate Op. 38 intensified with the coming of 1842, first taking the form of a four-hand ′piano arrangement which Clara began and then continued with her husband's aid.[3] Concurrently, the composer arranged to take the symphony on a joint concert tour with his wife, suggesting to Carl Koßmaly that interest in Op. 38 provided the occasion for the journey: '. . . I depart next month . . . as the result of an invitation from the philharmonic in Hamburg which wishes to perform my symphony and wants me together with my wife, naturally'.[4] In actual point of fact, it appears that Clara's return to the concert stage after her pregnancy and the early months of caring for her first child provided an equally strong impetus for the invitations. At one of the stops on the tour, Oldenburg, Clara played at court, while Robert to his chagrin was not even permitted to attend the concert. A request for Clara to extend her journey in order to perform in Copenhagen seems to have further hurt her husband's pride, though in diaries he put the

[2] Erler, *Briefe*, i. 271; either Schumann or perhaps Erler gives the wrong page for the first error, which appears on p. 1 not p. 5 of the part.

[3] The *Haushaltbücher* record the creation of this reduction during a visit from William Sterndale Bennett, beginning with a laconic comment on 17 January 1842, 'Clara is arranging my symphony', and ending with the equally brief note, 'the symphony reduction finished', pp. 205–7. The task irritated the composer, who wrote at one point, 'damned piano reduction', ibid. 206. Dörffel reports that the transcription appeared in June 1842, *Literarisches Verzeichnis*, p. 9, a date confirmed by Schumann in his letter to Eduard Krüger on 25 June 1842, Erler, *Briefe*, i. 280.

[4] Ibid. 275.

situation in the best light: 'Shall I neglect my talent in order to serve you as an escort on the trips? And you, shall you then let your talent go unused because I am tied to the journal and the piano? We have hit on the solution therefore that you take a female companion while I return to the child and my work.'[5] The reception of Op. 38 in Bremen under Friedrich Riem and in Hamburg under Friedrich Grund pleased the composer, of course,[6] but audiences and critics often regarded such occasions as concerts by Clara Schumann at which they also heard a symphony by her husband.

Apart from taking the Spring Symphony along on his personal appearances, Schumann secured some performances by petitioning various conductors and orchestras. Two days after the parts had appeared in print, he sent copies to the management of the *Concerts spirituels* in Vienna, requesting a performance which never came to pass.[7] The composer also sent letters to Carl Koßmaly, Wilhelm Taubert (Berlin), Carl Gollmick (Frankfurt), and Ferdinand David about performances, even inducing Moritz Hauptmann to place the piece before Ludwig Spohr in Kassel.[8] These efforts met with some success during the 1842-3 season and provided the occasion for detailed instructions to the various conductors derived from the composer's experience with performances during the previous year.

Schumann's letters to conductors of Op. 38 provide not only indications of how he thought it might be performed but also his developing sentiments about his scoring. By November of 1842 Schumann obviously wished to make some revisions in the instrumentation for the second Leipzig performance of the piece, as he says in his note to the conductor Ferdinand David:

The orchestra already knows the symphony, of course, and will surely find its way again quickly. And if you arrange to place another

---

[5] Rehberg, Walter and Paula, *Robert Schumann. Sein Leben und sein Werk*, 2nd edn (Zurich and Stuttgart, 1969), 25-55; an account of the episode can also be found in Berthold Litzmann, *Clara Schumann. Ein Künstlerleben nach Tagebüchern und Briefen*, 2nd edn, 3 vols (Leipzig, 1903-8), ii. 40-3.

[6] Schumann expressed satisfaction with both performances; see his letter to Theodor Töpken, Erler, *Briefe*, i. 276-7.

[7] Jansen, *Briefe*, pp. 209-10; also n. 262. It is possible that the set of parts donated by Schumann is now found in the Österreichische Nationalbibliothek, Musikabteilung, BA 368.

[8] Wolfgang Boetticher (ed.), *Briefe und Gedichte aus dem Album Robert und Clara Schumanns* (Leipzig, 1979), 74, 263.

orchestral piece, not too long or difficult, on the concert, time will also remain for rehearsing. I leave all of this to your friendly intentions and judgement. We will still discuss several passages in the symphony in person, especially one in the first movement. The

that the horns have [mm. 54–5, 58–9], has come out too muted everywhere I have heard the symphony. At the first performance it seemed to sound strong enough to me, and therefore I had it printed. I would rather use trombones, however, as I noted in my first sketches—in any event, we will try it one time with trombones.[9]

After hearing the second Leipzig performance on 3 November 1842, Schumann gave a longer list of instructions to Ludwig Spohr on 23 November, indicating page numbers of a manuscript score in which he had entered some corrections:

Even before Mr Hauptmann told me of your wish to receive [a copy of] my symphony, it had long been my intention to send you one, requesting your kindly verdict on it. Until now my efforts have been familiar to you only from smaller pieces—may this larger attempt afford you something of interest and enjoyment. I wrote the symphony at the end of winter in 1841, if I may say so, in the midst of that longing for spring which overpowers us even at the ripest age and overtakes us anew every year. I did not wish to depict or paint, but I believe that the period during which the symphony originated affected its formation and how it came to be just as it is. You will not find the symphony easy, but not altogether difficult. Allow me to indicate a few places which cause difficulties everywhere I have heard it. Immediately in the first three measures the first

in the trumpets often goes awry; at the last performance here, therefore, I made a

out of it in the parts, by means of which the entrance will certainly be more sure.—From *Più Vivace* in the introduction on, I like the tempo significantly faster right away.—A second alteration which I have written into the printed parts is noted on p. 56 of the score [mvt. I, mm. 317–8, 321–2] with small notes in the alto and tenor trombones. The place on p. 80 in the last measure [mvt. I, m. 484] also poses much difficulty, where the horns and trumpets never enter definitely enough with the theme.—The adagio presents no difficulties; but the first trio

---

[9] Jansen, *Briefe*, p. 222.[1]

in the scherzo does, where the figure

is usually slurred into

which I naturally do not want at all. Then, the violinists always forget the *p* on p. 127, measure 6 [mvt. III, m. 217], covering the brass completely. In the scherzo the *Coda* gives a great deal of trouble; it is also the most difficult thing in the symphony, and I ask for your particular solicitude if it is not to go indifferently. The last movement presents little of difficulty.

If I have taken the liberty of calling your attention to these passages, most esteemed Sir, it is because the mistakes which have been made in them have been repeated everywhere I have heard the symphony, and because I wished to prepare you specifically for them.[10]

Spohr performed the symphony on 18 January 1843 and returned the score to Schumann with comments two days later:

The work has also pleased me extraordinarily, and with every rehearsal—I held three very thorough ones—I was more attracted. If I should sketch more exactly my opinion of what I found particularly beautiful, it is first of all the magnificent development of the thematic figure at the beginning, but secondly, then, the whole scherzo with its distinctive, charming close, and the vigour and originality of the last movement. If I might allow myself to take exception, it would be first of all to the connection between the Adagio and Scherzo, for which I could discover no reason; furthermore there are too many blatant accompanimental figures in the adagio which envelop the cantilena too much (which appears idiomatic to me as a player of and composer for piano), and finally a phrase in the last allegro which begins with the tenor trombone solo, p. 172 [mvt. IV, m. 116] and does not harmonize with the character of the rest, and therefore probably led to the retransition for horns and solo flute, which also does not seem quite symphonic to me. But these are just my views, and my intuition can perhaps be mistaken![11]

Though this commentary criticizes some of Schumann's favourite gestures in the Spring Symphony, he was sufficiently proud of the general tone in Spohr's evaluation to retain the letter in a special album kept with Clara. His later revisions suggest that he took Spohr's comment about the tenor trombone in the last movement seriously.

10 Erler, *Briefe*, i. 290–1.   11 Boetticher, *Album*, p. 182.

The last of these lengthy communiqués about Op. 38 went to Wilhelm Taubert in Berlin, who led a performance on 14 February 1843. The conductor writes on 5 January:

I obtained the basic parts from Möser. (Must I return them to him, or are they still your property?) I still need at least 3 first, 3 second violins, 2 violas and 3 bass parts. If you can, include a fourth first and second violin part for a somewhat stronger doubling (10 first violins) which will depend on the exigencies of time however. Send me a score as soon as possible, accompanied by any tips you regard as necessary.[12]

In his reply on 10 January Schumann supplied an abundant commentary about the details of performance:

Right from the first trumpet entrance, I might wish as if it sounded from the heights, like a call to awaken—for what follows in the introduction I could maintain that everything grows verdant, that a butterfly even takes wing, and in the allegro that little by little everything appropriate to spring comes together. But these are fantasies which occurred to me *after* the completion of work; I will tell you only this of the last movement, that I would like to consider it as a *farewell* to spring, because I do not wish it to be taken too frivolously. Now to a couple of individual passages; take the score in hand and kindly follow along with me. I take the *Più vivace* in the introduction immediately *much* faster than the preceding, so that it leads unnoticed right into the *Allegro vivace*. You should have the horn passage appearing thus at sounding pitch [*Claviernoten*]

blown as strongly as possible [mvt. I, mm. 54–5, 58–9]; here in Leipzig I always hear it well, but in other orchestras quite faintly. Even more important is the same place after the *fff* following the middle of the movement where it appears

[mvt. I, mm. 317–18, 321–2]—should it come out too faintly, then double it with the *alto and tenor trombones*.

Take care also with the passage at the end, where horns and trumpets enter *marcato p* with the theme [mvt. I, m. 484], that they come out quite clearly. Otherwise the first movement and also the *Adagio* present no difficulties. The first trio of the Scherzo always creates even more

12 Ibid. 186–7.

trouble for me. They [the players] always slur the figure

so unclearly—if you have them play it as if the marking

were not even there, it will quickly go better—the remainder [should be] quite delicate and light. At the close of the same trio [mvt. III, m. 217], where flutes, oboes, bassoons, and clarinets have this

the strings usually exceed the *p*, which immediately follows an *f*. The most difficult thing in the entire symphony, however, is the *Coda* of the Scherzo; for my sake rehearse this passage quite often, my dear Taubert; I thank you for it quite sincerely. The last movement presents little of difficulty until the middle with the *flute cadenza*, which you will lead quite lightly and calmly back to the 1st tempo.[13]

Little over a year after he had first published the symphony, Schumann had very pronounced ideas about how he would further polish his orchestration. But he did not have any opportunity to publish a retouched version of Op. 38 until the spring of 1852, when he must have mentioned his desire for a printed score to Hermann Härtel during a visit to Leipzig in March.[14] True to his pragmatic method of orchestration, the composer did not send a copy for engraving to Härtel until he had heard his revisions at a subscription concert in Düsseldorf on 6 May 1852.[15] He dispatched the manuscript on 24 May with the following note, 'You will find enclosed the score of Manfred, only for the engraving of the overture at present, and also a completely corrected exemplar of the score for my 1st symphony, which you said you wished to have worked upon this 'summer', to my delight. . . .'[16] Härtel did indeed have the score engraved over the course of the summer, for Schumann

13 Erler, *Briefe*, i. 293–4.

14 The trip lasted from 5 March to 23 March; Schumann's negotiations with Härtel about the publication of the Manfred Overture can be found in Jansen, *Briefe*, p. 472.

15 The performance was well received, *Haushaltbücher*, pp. 797–8, n. 847.

16 Jansen, *Briefe*, pp. 472–3.

was able to correct the proofs on 28 September 1852.[17] He asked
Härtel for free copies of the print in a letter of 6 November,[18]
though the score was not available to the public until January
of 1853.[19]

REVISIONS FOR THE SECOND EDITION OF OP. 38

The score used to engrave the second edition of Op. 38 is now
housed in the Library of Congress under the siglum ML 31.H43a
N. 89; this copyist's manuscript bears the note 'revised for
printing 26 April 1852' in Schumann's hand on the last page, a
series of editorial queries, and engraver's markings dividing the
piece into sections suitable for the printed page. Linda Roesner
has suggested that this copy of the symphony does not date
from 1852 but from much earlier when the composer lived in
Leipzig.[20] The manuscript appears in the copyist's hand found
in the exposition from the last movement of the initial autograph,
a hand, moreover, unlike that of Schumann's Dresden and
Düsseldorf copyists. The similarity raises the legitimate question
of whether the engraver's copy is really the full score made for
Schumann in July 1841 and used from September to October
for proofreading the parts. But Schumann's original pencilled
note on the title page of the manuscript, 'rather mistake-ridden
copy, R. Sch.', implies that the composer probably did not use
this score to correct the parts for the first edition. In 1852 he
crossed out his original estimation of the copy on the title page
and wrote in ink, 'is to be revised before printing',[21] and he
deleted even this note when he had completely emended the
score.

The best evidence now indicates that the engraver's copy for
the second edition of Op. 38 originated in early 1842. Initially

[17] *Haushaltbücher*, p. 603.

[18] *Briefverzeichnis*, p. 536, no. 2125, ' . . . Bitte um einige Freiexemplare m. 1sten
Symphonie'.

[19] *Haushaltbücher*, p. 800, n. 862.

[20] See Linda Correll Roesner's 'Einige quellen- und textkritishe Bemerkungen zur
B-Dur-Sinfonie, Op. 38', forthcoming in the proceedings of the 1985 Düsseldorf
Schumann Symposium.

[21] 'ist vor d. Druck noch zu rediviren'; I rely on Edward Waters for this transcription
of a notation which I cannot entirely decipher, 'In All Forms & For All Mediums. *Music
Division Acquisitions*', *Quarterly Journal of the Library of Congress*, xxx (1973), 50.

Schumann had only one copy of the revised full score, for which he paid on 27 July 1841 and from which he corrected the printed parts in October 1841. When conductors requested a copy of the score for performances, he sent at first this unique manuscript (and therefore he kept his diary of performances in the obsolete autograph rather than in a working score constantly in transit). As early as the autumn of 1841, however, the composer found this arrangement unsatisfactory, as a letter to Albert Schiffner of Dresden on 9 November discloses:

> Unfortunately, at the moment I do not have the score of my symphony at home. Herr Capellmeister Chélard in Weimar asked for it, because he wishes to perform it during the next few weeks. Will Herr M.[usik] D.[irektor] Hartung, to whom you will give my best, kindly wait until after the performance in Weimar? On the other hand, I myself would certainly prefer that he become acquainted with the work from the score. Let us do it this way: I will write to you at the end of this month about the status of the performance in Weimar, and meanwhile you will ask Herr M. D. Hartung to postpone the public performance a bit longer.[22]

As Schumann arranged for more performances, he must have required a second manuscript score. He may have referred to the manufacture of such a copy obliquely in a letter to Theodore Lallemant on 18 February 1842 while discussing the approaching performance in Hamburg: 'The copyist is at fault for the delay; and I also have been so sick for the past 14 days that the whole trip was thrown into doubt.'[23] The composer would not likely refer to the copying of parts in this communication, because printed parts were available. He must be speaking of a second manuscript score copied in haste (with the many mistakes his note on the title page indicates?) by his only known Leipzig scribe, C. Brückner,[24] for the joint tour in February and March. Because Schumann possessed two full scores of the symphony

[22] Ludwig Schmidt, 'Unbekannte Musikerbriefe', NZfM, lxvii (1900), 142; Johann Wilhelm Hartung conducted the Dresden Stadtkapelle and Prince Maximillian's regimental Kapelle as well.

[23] Jansen, Briefe, p. 213.

[24] Nauhaus lists Brückner as a music teacher in Leipzig; Schumann first mentions him in November 1840 and uses him as late as 1845 during a visit to Leipzig. The composer also seems to have bought staff paper from Brückner from time to time. See Haushaltbücher, p. 845.

after this tour, he could send one to Taubert in Berlin on 10 January 1843, while Spohr used the other score in Kassel, returning it on 20 January. The engraver's copy in the Library of Congress appears to be the copy sent to Kassel: Roesner has observed that the page numbers cited in Schumann's letter to Spohr match those in the Library of Congress manuscript.[25]

The engraver's copy yields a concrete record of Schumann's cumulative revision of the Spring Symphony over the period of a decade. The changes speak to almost all the points he raised with David, Spohr, and Taubert, and they often follow principles familiar from Schumann's earlier work on the orchestration of the piece. The reinforcement of key rhetorical figures given to the brass at crucial junctures seems chief among the composer's concerns in his letters to various conductors, and the engraver's copy speaks directly to these. Schumann supplies a defiant answer to Spohr's objections about the character of the trombone entrance in measure 116 of the fourth movement: he adds the bass trombone (p. 172 of the engraver's copy) to the tenor in the engraver's copy, leaving no doubt about the heraldic effect he had in mind. The reinforcement of the solo horns by trombones in measures 317–18 and 321–2 of the first movement on pages 36–7 of the corrected manuscript, mentioned in all of

---

[25] One other manuscript score of the symphony, British Museum Additional MS 31803, deserves passing mention. The copyist's hand here does not seem related to that in other manuscripts directly associated with the composer, at least any known to me personally. None the less, certain aspects of this score suggest a close relationship to the autograph and also to the engraver's manuscript. For instance, the instruments in Add. 31803 appear in the order peculiar to Schumann's scores, the version of the text seems to reproduce that of the printed parts (with fewer mistakes and disagreements in articulation, however), and one of Schumann's notes in the autograph (75ᵛ), 'bei der Wiederholung hat die *Bratsche* wie unten steht', is repeated almost verbatim in the British Museum copy, even to the underlining. The recapitulation of the main theme in Add. 31803 also follows a numbering scheme similar to that suggested in the autograph on 97ᵛ. Add. 31803, then, is most likely a copy of the lost manuscript score from which Schumann corrected his parts, but we do not know its precise provenance. Roesner has said privately that the manuscript score may be connected with William Sterndale Bennett, who visited the Schumanns just at the time Clara was making the four-hand reduction of the Op. 38. Much of Bennett's library did come into the hands of Julian Marshall, whose collection, purchased by the British Museum in 1880–1, included Add. 31803. For further information, see *Catalogue of Additions to the Manuscripts in the British Museum in the Years MDCCCLXXVI–MDCCCLXXXI* (London, 1882), 228; and Arthur Searle, 'Julian Marshall and the British Museum: Music Collecting in the Later Nineteenth Century', *British Library Journal*, ii (1985), 67–87.

his communications, also becomes an official part of the text in the print of the full score, bringing the long history of this passage to a close. Schumann had imagined the figure played by horns and trombones in his sketch ('Corni u. T.' 6^r, system 6), but he scored it for the trombones alone in the autograph (40^r). His private query about 'trombone' at the bottom of this page in the autograph suggests some unease about the assignment, and he gives the passage to the horns in the 1841 print. The combination of the two colours in the 1853 version and its concomitant reinforcement of the gesture provides a good instance of the way in which Schumann's thinking about some passages unfolded over a long period of time as a result of repeated experimentation. As we have seen earlier, his rehearings often confirm the aural image projected originally in his sketches.

Yet another example of melodic reinforcement appears in measures 151–60 of the oboe and clarinet parts for the fourth movement, with the latter displayed in both 1841 and 1853 printed versions (Ex. 5.1). The general texture of the surrounding voices is full in this passage: the strings play tremolo chords, the timpani, horns, and flutes reinforce them during every solo by the first oboe, while the bassoons articulate the supporting bass throughout. The many instruments accompanying the first oboe must have obscured its line, for Schumann decided to drop the clarinet chords of the 1841 print and reinforce the first oboe solo with the first clarinet in the 1853 print. Schumann recorded these revisions as part of the engraver's copy on pages 177–9. The composer never tired of recasting his melodies in the strong light praised by Kahlert's review of Op. 38, and in this sense all of his changes in orchestration after the initial scoring present a picture of consistent progress towards a clearly defined goal.

According to later, probably spurious accounts, Schumann omitted from the final print one significant alteration in orchestration and pitch syntax which he allegedly desired. In most versions of the story concerning changes in the initial pitch of the opening fanfare, writers recount Jansen's report that 'when [Schumann] handed over a copy of the score which appeared in 1853 to Verhulst, he remarked that he was still sorry to have altered the beginning motto. For this reason Verhulst always performed [the beginning of] the symphony in its original

Example 5.1   Schumann, Op. 38, mvt. 4, oboe and clarinet parts for mm. 151–60 in 1841 and 1853 prints

version.'[26] Verhulst's anecdote rings untrue. By the time Schumann revised the score of Op. 38 in 1852 he had already written specifically for valved horns and trumpets in his Third Symphony (composed during 1850); he could easily have called for them in his revised score of Op. 38 and altered the opening motto. And the orchestral parts of the first edition could have been changed accordingly in rehearsals. It may be that Schumann declined to alter his opening in the 1853 print because he came to regard a beginning on D as essential to the tonal logic of his piece. In the first layer of sketching he begins the motto on D, and in logical consequence D persists as an alternate tonal centre

[26] F. Gustav Jansen, *Die Davidsbündler: aus Robert Schumanns Sturm- und Drangperiode* (Leipzig, 1883), p. 245, n. 176. Ostensibly Schumann presented a copy of the score to Verhulst during a tour to the Netherlands at the end of 1853, see the *Haushaltbücher*, pp. 642–3.

to B flat in the first movement and throughout most of the symphony. The display of the ambiguity between D and B flat at the very outset of the first movement provides a motivation for the tonal progress that follows.

Schumann did take the occasion of the second edition to revise details of phrasing and slurring in some passages with an eye to repairing the inconsistent articulation in the printed parts of the first edition. A good instance of such a revision comes in a passage at the end of the first movement, measures 452–63. Ex. 5.2a shows this passage in the 1841 print, and Ex. 5.2b displays the same music as revised in the 1853 edition. If we compare the two versions, we see that instruments playing the same line or identical rhythms in the 1841 print are sometimes slurred quite differently; in general, the slurs in the woodwinds create much longer phrases, while the slurs in the string parts tend to group short motives. The 1853 full score equalizes much of the wind and string slurring, and conforms the winds for the most part to the shorter slurs in the strings. For this reason the phrasing of measures 452–63 in the second edition is more articulate and lends more clarity to rhythmic patterns in this heavily scored passage.

The mechanism for this kind of revision involves Schumann's interplay with the editors at Breitkopf. His alterations of slurring for this passage in the engraver's copy (pp. 76–7) display his attempt to equalize articulation for the sake of consistency, but he does not achieve uniformity. Instead, Breitkopf's editor or perhaps the engraver, following the spirit of Schumann's alterations if not the letter, brings the lines into better agreement. The composer must have paid special attention to passages that he had explicitly corrected in his score as he proofread the second edition, and he seems to have sanctioned the process of equalization in this and other sections of the text. The full score presents an extremely careful recension of the piece, and we can say with some justification that the composer viewed the 1853 print as an improvement over the earlier edition.

Schumann's interest in precise and reasonable instructions to the performers of Op. 38 can be seen again in his concern with the temporal aspects of his second edition. When revising the autograph version of Op. 38 to produce the first edition the composer concentrated on rendering certain internal changes of

Example 5.2a   Schumann, Op. 38, mvt. 1, slurring in mm. 452–63 of
the 1841 print

Example 5.2*b*   Schumann, Op. 38, mvt. 1, slurring in mm. 452–63 of the 1853 print

tempo automatic by translating them into proportional note values in an unvarying time signature, avoiding any possible misreading on the part of the performers and also preventing problems of ensemble. In the printed score precision in the temporal realm assumes the shape of altered metronome markings. Table 12 shows that Schumann reduced the speed of the beat for the first, third, and fourth movements of Op. 38 in the second edition. Moreover these changes do not appear in the engraver's manuscript but only in the final print, suggesting that they came at the very end of Schumann's continual polishing and revision of the piece. Schumann reports in correspondence to Ferdinand Böhme during February 1853 on the state of his own metronome:

> Do you have a correct metronome? . . . Mine is correct. There are as many beats in a minute as indicated by the number upon which the weight is placed, if upon 50 then 50 beats in a minute, upon 60 = 60. And this is the test, in so far as I know, of accuracy. Do you want to compare your metronome, perhaps, to this standard?[27]

It seems unlikely in light of Schumann's discussion that he would be misled by a defective metronome, or that he possessed a faulty one during this time.[28] If Schumann's readings are reliable, then the revised metronome markings for the second edition of Op. 38 imply that the composer came to regard the indications for some movements in the first edition as too rapid.

It may well be that the Gewandhaus Orchestra under Mendelssohn played the piece at the fast tempi marked in the first edition (though some of the speeds are extreme). But Schumann came to realize the cost of velocity: his repeated complaints to David, Spohr, and Taubert about the inarticulate central rhythmic motive of the first trio probably resulted from the fast tempi indicated for the third movement in the first printed edition. For this reason, Schumann opts to correct the problem by drastically reducing of metronome markings rather than changing the articulation for the central figure of the first trio, as he suggests in his letters. Schumann's experience with ensembles

---

[27] Jansen, *Briefe*, p. 365.

[28] Jansen writes that Schumann's metronome was found to be inaccurate after his death, but fails to give the source of his information, ibid. 529, n. 445. Brian Schlotel suggests one possible source for Jansen's assertion in 'Schumann and the Metronome', *Robert Schumann: The Man and His Music*, ed. Alan Walker (London, 1972), 110. In the light of Schumann's letter Jansen's notion seems less than likely.

TABLE 12   *Comparison of metronome markings in the two editions of Op. 38*

1841 print	Movement	1853 print
Andante (♩ = 76)	I	Andante (♩ = 66)
Allegro molto vivace (♩ = 152)		Allegro molto vivace (♩ = 120)
Larghetto (♪ = 66)	II	Larghetto (♪ = 66)
Molto vivace (♩. = 138)	III	Molto vivace (♩. = 88)
Molto più vivace (♩ = 144)		Molto più vivace (♩ = 108)
Allegro animato e grazioso (♩ = 116)	IV	Allegro animato e grazioso (♩ = 100)

distinctly less co-ordinated than the Leipzig orchestra under Mendelssohn convinced him that his original tempi were not universally appropriate. The same was true for another work given its first performance in Leipzig and designed for that ensemble, the *Ouverture, Scherzo und Finale*; again Schumann radically reduced the metronome markings between the publication of the parts of the first edition and the second edition in score some years later.[29] And a brief glance at the metronome markings for the only other Schumann symphony given its première in Leipzig under Mendelssohn, the Second Symphony, also reveals some very fast tempi.[30]

[29] See 'Robert Schumann: The Creation of the Symphonic Works' (PhD dissertation, University of Chicago, 1980), 177–8; some of the changes are also mentioned in my article, 'Schumann, Popularity and the Overture, Scherzo and Finale, Op. 52', *Musical Quarterly*, lxix (1983), 17–18.

[30] Eduard Krüger calls the marking for the last movement in his review 'ungeheuer und unverständlich rasch' and observes that 170 does not even exist on the metronome, 'Robert Schumann, Zweite Symphonie', *AMZ*, l (1848), col. 373. Michael Struck summarizes briefly the various divergent opinions about Schumann's metronome markings in his later works, and recounts the belief of some that the slower tempi result from an altered perception of time owing to mental impairment, *Die umstrittenen späten Instrumentalwerke Schumanns: Untersuchungen zur Entstehung, Struktur und Rezeption* (Hamburg, 1984), 622. The letter to Böhme about the metronome speaks plainly to Schumann's sanity on these matters. And if we argue that Schumann's perception of time changed at the end of his life, we will need to explain why the altered perception applied to some movements in Op. 38 and not to others. I suggest it would be easier to discard the completely undemonstrated (and unsupportable?) notion that Schumann's later pieces contain symptoms of his last illness.

The final revision in the metronome markings for Op. 38 suggests the significant implications of the empirical procedure Schumann devised as a young man for dealing with the revision of orchestral pieces: it depended heavily on the specific context of performance from which the composer judged results. For his first four orchestral works, Opp. 38, 52, 61, and 120, Schumann initially selected the Gewandhaus as a model of the symphony orchestra. Wasielewski leaves a clear account of how Mendelssohn and David treated Schumann during the première of the Second Symphony in 1846:

So far as technique was concerned, the performance presented difficulties, specifically for the violins and woodwinds, which were unheard of at that time and which caused much resistance on the part of many players. Mendelssohn took pains through careful rehearsals that all went well, and David, who was given a hard nut to crack in the chains of trills in the Adagio, did not rest until the ensemble of the violins was as precise as it was pure and clean.[31]

This tale has many points of similarity to Dörffel's chronicle about the première of the Spring Symphony. Mendelssohn's solicitous attitude towards Schumann's orchestral works and his meticulous attention to their rehearsal helped his friend to gain public exposure for each piece, to interest publishers, and to refine his orchestration. The process led the composer to tailor his symphonies closely to the qualities of the Gewandhaus orchestra. When Schumann became better acquainted with the orchestral world outside of Leipzig, he revised certain features of his symphonies to accommodate wider use. The context of his activity was limited, none the less; his pieces remained intimately associated with the mid-nineteenth-century German philharmonic and its relatively small number of players.

Epilogue

I have stressed Schumann's empirical process of scoring Op. 38 at such great length, in part because it provides the key to understanding the later reception of his orchestration. Critics and conductors in Schumann's clearly defined symphonic world found the Spring Symphony to be well scored, and for this

[31] Wilhelm Joseph von Wasielewski, *Schumanniana* (Bonn, 1883), 17.

reason among others, including its cohesive structure and imaginative ideas, it occupied a secure place in the concert repertory of many European musical centres. Substantial criticism of Schumann's instrumentation did not surface until a whole generation after the composition of Op. 38 in the writings of musicians like Tchaikovsky:

A great connoisseur of all the qualities and most subtle resources of his favourite instrument—the piano—he is an inimitable master in the art of drawing out the rich, luxuriant sonority of this miniature orchestra. But apparently Schumann could never call forth the inexhaustible treasures of the modern orchestra. . . . It is said that he wrote [his First Symphony] under the strong influence and personal guidance of Mendelssohn. The traces of this influence are not, however, apparent. Schumann, in his First Symphony, with all its positive and negative qualities, shows more strength and capability and greater individuality than Mendelssohn. On the one hand, wealth of imagination, simplicity of design, the plasticity of a Beethoven in its fundamental form; on the other, a lack of colour, obscurity, and a disregard of attractive details of orchestration—this is what we find in Schumann's first essay in symphonic writing.[32]

Schumann could not 'call forth' the treasures of Tchaikovsky's 'modern orchestra' because he did not have it at his disposal; in following an empirical method he could only score for the ensemble at hand. The larger orchestra to which Tchaikovsky refers appeared after Schumann's time under the demands of composers like Wagner. For example, the Gewandhaus orchestra, which numbered 49 players in 1839 (a number retained during Schumann's residence in Leipzig), grew to about 60 players in 1860, 72 in 1881, and 86 by 1896. At the turn of the century symphony orchestras in large cities generally featured approximately 100 players. Only a small part of this increase resulted from the addition of new wind instruments to the orchestra; most of the extra players can be found in vastly expanded string sections. The newly enlarged string section altered the balances in Schumann's symphonies, giving rise to Felix Weingartner's widely repeated criticisms:

[32] Rosa Newmarch, *Tchaikovsky: His Life and Works, with Extracts from His Writings, and the Diary of His Tour Abroad in 1888* (Bodley Head, New York, 1900; reprinted New York, 1969), 135–6.

He almost always works with full material and does not exert himself to work out the lines according to the character of the individual instruments. With an almost childlike naïveté he imagines he can achieve fullness and power through doubling. Therefore, the tonal effect is viscous and awkward, the colours grey on grey, the most important voices cannot be heard if they are played according to his indications, and a true forte is for the most part as impossible as a true piano. I recommend at performances a ruthless procedure with these constrictions, not to modernize the orchestration by reinforcement but to achieve transparency by deleting all superfluous parts. I have obtained profitable results from this practice. Certainly, Schumann's orchestration will not gain brilliance or colourfulness this way, but [it will gain] clarity, and this is always an advantage over the pasty effect of the original.[33]

Arnold Schoenberg suggests that Weingartner's remarks participate in the 'fight between the Wagnerian "New German" School and the Schumann–Brahmsian–Academic–Classicist School',[34] but I find the conductor's reaction honest given the circumstances under which he listened. Weingartner, along with many other conductors of his time, frequently reorchestrated works by earlier composers. For instance, he devotes a whole book to his retouching of Beethoven's symphonies, explaining in his foreword that certain reinstrumentations and rewriting of parts could be justified to promote more 'clarity'.[35] If we insist on performing Schumann's First Symphony with modern orchestral forces, we might reasonably submit to Weingartner's retouchings.

It seems incredible that Weingartner did not imagine an alternative means of achieving proper balance in Schumann's orchestration: reducing the proportions of the ensemble to resemble those for which the composer so meticulously fashioned his First Symphony. If we adopted this practice, orchestras playing Schumann would not exceed Mendelssohn's or Taubert's optimistic maximum ensemble of around fifty players. The relatively low or middling tessitura for the more colourful wind parts could then be distinguished amidst the frequent string doubling, and the fullness Schumann hoped to achieve would

---

[33] Felix Weingartner, *Die Symphonie nach Beethoven*, 3rd edn. (Leipzig, 1909), 29.

[34] Arnold Schoenberg, *Style and Idea* (New York, 1950), 37.

[35] Felix Weingartner, *Ratschläge für Aufführungen Klassischer Symphonien*, 4th edn. (Wiesbaden, 1958), iii–xi.

be preserved. As Weingartner implies, we will still hear a darkly coloured sound, one that Schumann evidently preferred. This heavy, rich sonority lies at the heart of a symphonic tradition which includes Brahms and later Sibelius. Brahms in particular invests much creative energy translating Schumann's textures into orchestrations effective with the larger ensemble at the disposal of composers toward the end of the nineteenth century.

I have also stressed Schumann's empirical approach because it provides the link between the compositional practice of his first decade and the creative process he employed in subsequent years. Schumann spent most of his career before 1841 applying his empirical method to formal levels of music. Linda Roesner has documented this compositional process for the *Davidsbündler-tänze*, Rufus Hallmark for *Dichterliebe*, and Barbara Turchin for *Liederkreis*, Op. 39.[36] These pieces are not collections of mini-atures, they are experiments in large formal design. The composer, wishing to avoid conventional formal arrangements, derives the shape of each by trial and error, writing the individual sections and then experimenting with the most psychologically satisfying order, often discarding or adding material in the process. Such a procedure does not by any means exclude logical coherence, for the relationship of the various parts derives to some extent from the interweaving of motives and keys. The integrity of the whole, promoted by this interweaving, also originates in patterns of dramatic juxtaposition motivated by an overriding, often literary concept. The specific form develops empirically within the intellectual framework provided by the central conceit.

When Schumann turned to the symphony he applied his empirical approach not to formal matters but to some aspects of material and to orchestration. He selected Schubert's symphonic manner partly on the basis of its proven success with the Leipzig audience and on the basis of his own experience at rehearsals of the Great C-major. The process of change in the opening fanfare of his own symphony, the alteration of the coda to the first

[36] See Linda Correll Roesner, 'The Sources for Schumann's *Davidsbündlertänze*, Op. 6: Composition, Textual Problems, and the Role of the Composer as Editor', *Mendelssohn and Schumann: Essays on Their Music and Its Context* (Durham, NC, 1984), 53–70; Rufus Hallmark, 'The Sketches for *Dichterliebe*', *19th Century Music*, i (1977), 110–36; Barbara Turchin, 'Robert Schumann's Song Cycles: The Cycle within the Song', *19th Century Music* viii (1985), 236–43.

movement, the rearrangement of the various ornamental gestures in the last movement, and the pervasive reworking of texture all result from Schumann's observation of the repeated performances to which the symphony was subjected before it appeared in print. We should not be surprised to find an empirical compositional process linking Schumann's early and later music; the composer approached the Spring Symphony with some of the devices he had developed as a young man for the G-minor Symphony, written at the same time as the first experimental piano pieces. Schumann's tendency to compose some aspects of his music by trial and error is one of his important strengths as a composer. I am reminded in this respect of Jacques Barzun's characterization of nineteenth-century art as drawing on concrete experience instead of abstractions:

for substance [the romanticists] turned to the world about and within them; they tried to meet the claims of every existing reality, both internal and external. . . . As against poetic diction and 'noble' words, the romanticists admitted all words, as against the exclusive use of a selected Graeco-Roman mythology, they took in the Celtic and Germanic; as against the uniform setting and tone of classical tragedy, they studied and observed diversities known as 'local colour.' As against the antique subjects and the set scale of pictorial merits prescribed by the Academy, they took in the whole world, seen and unseen, and the whole range of colours. As against the academic rules prohibiting the use of certain chords, tonalities, and modulations, they sought to use and give shape to all manageable combinations of sound.[37]

The attractiveness of Schumann's compositions originates not just a little in his willingness 'to study and observe' the concrete results of his writing.

The interplay between Schumann's empiricism and his latent neoclassicism produces the central tension of the piece. In Op. 38 Schumann creates for the first time his peculiar version of the classic–romantic synthesis which would have such a profound effect on the symphonies of Brahms and Tchaikovsky. Because the Spring Symphony represents Schumann's earliest completed attempt at such a synthesis in the orchestral realm, its components—the 'new' Schubertian manner, architectonic form, and empirically conditioned sonority and gesture—jostle

[37] Jacques Barzun, *Classic, Romantic and Modern* (New York, 1961), 59–60.

one another just a bit, yielding the exuberance and vitality that immediately attracted audiences in Schumann's time and that continue to hold listeners today.

References

MANUSCRIPT SOURCES

British Museum, London
: Additional MS 31803, copy of Op. 38 from the mid-1840s (?), provenance unknown.

Deutsche Staatsbibliothek, Berlin
: Mus. ms. 1256/40, reduction of an excerpt from Beethoven's Ninth Symphony, first movement, in Schumann's hand.

Gesellschaft der Musikfreunde, Vienna
: A-289, autograph of the *Ouvertüre, Scherzo und Finale*, Op. 52, with portions in the hand of Clara Schumann and a copyist.

Library of Congress, Washington, D.C.
: ML 96.S415 Case, autograph of the first version of Op. 38, with portions in copyist's hand.
: ML 31, H43a N. 89, copy of Op. 38 used to engrave the second edition.

Staatsbibliothek Preußischer Kulturbesitz, Berlin
: Mus. ms. auto. Schumann 12, autograph of Op. 97 with portions in copyist's hand, used to engrave the first edition.

Universitätsbibliothek, Bonn
: Schumann 15 (formerly Skizzenbuch III, Wiede 11/301c), autograph miscellany containing early symphonic sketches.
: Schumann 16 (formerly Skizzenbuch IV, Wiede 11/301d), autograph miscellany containing Schumann's reductions of Beethoven's Fourth Symphony, second movement, and the Lenore Overture No. 3.
: Schuman 19, sketches for a 'Symphonie (1840)' and a 'Symphonie (1841)', as well as a partial score of the latter.

Wiede Collection   11/37, autograph score of G-minor Symphony, first movement, dating from autumn 1832.

———   11/300a, autograph score of G-minor Symphony, first movement, fair copy of 11/300b.

———   11/300b, autograph score of G-minor Symphony, first and second movements, transitional copy dating from January (?) 1833.

———   11/300c, autograph score of G-minor Symphony, second movement, fair copy of 11/300b.

———   11/300d, autograph miscellany of sketches and some scoring for G-minor Symphony.

PUBLISHED WORKS

Abraham, Gerald: 'Schumann's *Jugendsinfonie* in G Minor', *Musical Quarterly*, xxxvii (1951), 45–60.
——— A Hundred Years of Music, 4th edn. (London, 1974).
Barzun, Jacques, *Classic, Romantic and Modern* (New York, 1961)
Beethoven, Ludwig van, *Sinfonio Nr. 3, Es-dur*, Op. 55, perf. Collegium aurem (Deutsche Harmonia Mundi, matrix no. IC 065–99–629 QB, 1976).
Berlioz, Hector: *Fantastic Symphony*, ed. Edward T. Cone (New York, 1971).
——— *Memoirs of Hector Berlioz, Member of the French Institute, including his travels in Italy, Germany, Russia and England, 1803–1865*, trans. David Cairns (New York, 1969), 295–9.
Boetticher, Wolfgang (ed.), *Briefe und Gedichte aus dem Album Robert und Clara Schumanns* (Leipzig, 1979).
——— 'Robert Schumann an Seine Königliche Majestät', *Die Musik*, xxxiii (1940), 58–65.
——— *Robert Schumann: Einführung in Persönlichkeit und Werk* (Berlin, 1941).
Catalogue of Additions to the Manuscripts in the British Museum in the Years MDCCCLXXVI–MDCCCLXXXI (London, 1882)
Deutsch, Otto Erich: 'The Discovery of Schubert's Great C-Major Symphony: A Story in Fifteen Letters', *Musical Quarterly* xxxviii (1952), 528–33.
Dörffel, Alfred: *Geschichte der Gewandhausconcerte zu Leipzig vom*

25. *November 1781 bis 25. November 1881*, 2 vols. (Leipzig, 1884).
——*Literarisches Verzeichnis der im Druck erschienenen Tonwerke von Robert Schumann*, supplement to *Musikalisches Wochenblatt*, i (1870).
Dz.: 'Zweites Concert der Euterpe, den 15. Novbr.', *NZfM*, xv (1841), 172.
Eckhardt, Julius: *Ferdinand David und die Familie Mendelssohn-Bartholdy* (Leipzig, 1888).
Eismann, Georg: 'Nachweis der internationalen Standorte von Noten-autographen Robert Schumanns', *Sammelbände der Robert-Schumann-Gesellschaft*, ii (1966), 7–37.
Finson, Jon W.: 'Robert Schumann: The Creation of the Symphonic Works' (PhD dissertation, University of Chicago, 1980)
——'Schumann and Shakespeare', in Jon W. Finson and R. Larry Todd (eds.) *Mendelssohn and Schumann: Essays on Their Music and Its Context*, (Durham, NC, 1984), 125–36.
——'Schumann, Popularity, and the Overture, Scherzo and Finale, Op. 52', *Musical Quarterly*, lxix (1983), 1–26.
——'The Sketches for Robert Schumann's C Minor Symphony', *Journal of Musicology*, i (1982), 395–418.
——'The Sketches for the Fourth Movement of Schumann's Second Symphony, Op. 61.', *Journal of the American Musicological Society*, xxxix (1986), pp. 143–68.
Gossett, Philip: 'Beethoven's Sixth Symphony: Sketches for the First Movement', *Journal of the American Musicological Society*, xxvii (1974), 248–84.
Graßner, Ferdinand Simon: *Partiturkenntniß, ein Leitfaden zum Selbstun-terrichte für angehende Tonsetzer, oder solche, welche Arrangiren, Partiturlesen lernen oder sich zu Dirigenten von Orchestern oder Militärmusiken bilden wollen*, 2nd edn., 2 vols. (Karlsruhe, 1842).
Hallmark, Rufus: 'A Sketch Leaf for Schumann's D-Minor Symphony', in Jon W. Finson and R. Larry Todd (eds.) *Mendelssohn and Schumann: Essays on Their Music and Its Context*, (Durham, NC, 1984), 39–51.
——'The Sketches for *Dichterliebe*', *19th Century Music*, i (1977), 110–36.
Hofmann, Kurt: *Die Erstdrucke der Werke von Robert Schumann* (Tutzing, 1979).
Jansen, F. Gustav: *Die Davidsbündler: aus Robert Schumann's Sturm- und Drangperiode* (Leipzig, 1883).
Kahlert, August: '*Robert Schumann*: Symphonie für grosses Orchester, Componirt von——. Op. 38. Leipzig, bei Breitkopf & Härtel. Preis 6 Thlr., 15 Ngr., *AMZ*, xliv (1842), cols. 265–71.
Kapp, Reinhard: *Studien zum Spätwerk Robert Schumanns* (Tutzing, 1984).

Kinsky, Georg: *Musikhistorisches Museum von Wilhelm Heyer in Cöln*, 4 vols. (Cologne, 1916).

—— *Versteigerung von Musiker-Autographen aus dem Nachlaß des Herrn Kommerzienrates Wilhelm Heyer in Köln . . . Montag, den 6. und Dienstag, den 7. Dezember 1926 . . . durch Ernst Henrici & Leo Liepmannssohn. Antiquariat . . . Berlin.*

Koury, Daniel J.: *Orchestral Performance Practices in the Nineteenth Century: Size, Proportions, and Seating* (Ann Arbor, 1986).

Krüger, Eduard: 'Robert Schumann, Zweite Symphonie', *AMZ*, l (1848), cols. 353–7, 369–73.

'Leipzig (Beschluss)', *AMZ* xliii (1841), cols. 330–4.

Litzmann, Berthold: *Clara Schumann: Ein Künstlerleben nach Tagebüchern und Briefen*, 2nd edn., 3 vols. (Leipzig, 1903–8).

Mayeda, Akio: 'Die Skizzen Robert Schumanns als stillkritische Erkenntnisquelle', *Robert Schumann—Ein romantisches Erbe in neuer Forschung* (Mainz, London, New York, Tokyo, 1984), 119–39.

Newcomb, Anthony: 'Schumann and Late Eighteenth-Century Narrative Strategies', *19th Century Music*, xi (1987), 164–74.

Newmarch, Rosa: *Tchaikovsky: His Life and Works, with Extracts from His Writings, and the Diary of His Tour Abroad in 1888* (The Bodley Head, New York, 1900; reprinted New York, 1969).

Ostwald, Peter: *Schumann: The Inner Voices of a Musical Genius* (Boston, 1985)

Plantinga, Leon B.: *Schumann as Critic* (New Haven and London, 1967).

—— 'Schumann's Critical Reaction to Mendelssohn', in Jon W. Finson and R. Larry Todd (eds.) *Mendelssohn and Schumann: Essays on Their Music and Its Context* (Durham, NC, 1984), 11–19.

Ratz, Erwin: *Einführung in die musikalische Formenlehre: über Formprinzipien in den Inventionen und Fugen J. S. Bachs und ihre Bedeutung für die Kompositionstechnik Beethovens*, 3rd edn. (Vienna, 1973).

Rehberg, Walter and Rehberg, Paula: *Robert Schumann. Sein Leben und sein Werk*, 2nd edn. (Zurich and Stuttgart, 1969).

Robert Schumann. Manuskripte, Briefe, Schumanniana, Katalog Nr. 188 (Tutzing, 1974).

Roesner, Linda Correll: 'Studies in Schumann Manuscripts: With Particular Reference to Sources Transmitting Instrumental Works in the Large Forms', 2 vols. (PhD dissertation, New York University, 1973).

—— 'The Sources for Schumann's *Davidsbündlertänze*, Op. 6: Composition, Textual Problems, and the Role of Composer as Editor', *Mendelssohn and Schumann: Essays on Their Music and Its Context* (Durham, NC, 1984).

—— 'Einige quellen- und textkritishe Bemerkungen zur B-Dur-Sinfonie, Op. 38', forthcoming in the proceedings of the 1985 Düsseldorf Schumann Symposium.

Schlotel, Brian: 'Schumann and the Metronome', in Alan Walker (ed.) *Robert Schumann: The Man and His Music* (London, 1972), 109–19.

Schmidt, Ludwig: 'Unbekannte Musikerbriefe', *NZfM*, lxvii (1900), 141–2.

Schoenberg, Arnold: *Style and Idea* (New York, 1950).

Schumann, Eugenie: *Robert Schumann. Ein Lebensbild meines Vaters* (Leipzig, 1931).

Schumann, Robert: ' "Aus dem Leben eines Künstlers." Phantastische Symphonie in 5 Abtheilungen von Hector Berlioz', *NZfM*, iii (1835), 1–2, 33–5, 37–8, 41–51.

—— 'Concertouverturen für Orchester', *NZfM* x (1839).

—— *Exercices. Etüden in Form freier Variationen über ein Thema von Beethoven*, ed. Robert Münster (Munich, 1976).

—— 'Fragmente aus Leipzig', *NZfM*, vi (1837), 209.

—— *Haushaltbücher*, ed. Gerd Nauhaus, 2 parts (Leipzig, 1982).

—— *Jugendbriefe von Robert Schumann*, ed. Clara Schumann, 2nd edn. (Leipzig, 1886).

—— 'Neue Symphonieen für Orchester', *NZfM* xi (1839), 1.

—— Die Priessymphonie, *NZfM* v (1836), 147–8, 151–2.

—— *Robert Schumanns Briefe, Neue Folge*, ed. F. Gustav Jansen, 2nd edn. (Leipzig, 1904).

—— *Robert Schumann's Leben aus seinen Briefen geschildert*, ed. Hermann Erler, 2nd edn., 2 vols. (Berlin, 1887).

—— 'Rückblick auf das Leipziger Musikleben im Winter 1837–1838', *NZfM* viii (1838), 115

—— *Selbstbiographische Notizen Facsimile*, ed. Martin Schoppe (Zwickau, [n.d.])

—— 'Die 7te Symphonie von Franz Schubert', *NZfM* xii (1840), 81–3.

—— *Sinfonie G-Moll für Orchester*, ed. Marc Andrae (Frankfurt, New York, and London, 1972).

—— 'Schwärmbriefe. Eusebius an Chaira', *NZfM* iii (1835), 126–7.

—— 'Symphonieen', *NZfM* vii (1837), 111–12.

—— *Symphony, Opus 38* (New York, 1967).

—— *Tagebücher*, ed. Georg Eismann (Leipzig, 1971).

Schwarz, Werner: 'Eine Musikerfreundschaft des 19. Jahrhunderts', in Christoph Helmut Mahling (ed.) *Zum 70. Geburtstag von Joseph Müller-Blattau* (Kassel, 1960), 282–303.

Searle, Arthur: 'Julian Marshall and the British Museum: Music

Collecting in the Later Nineteenth Century', *British Library Journal*, ii (1985), 67–87.

Struck, Michael: *Die umstrittenen späten Instrumentalwerke Schumanns: Untersuchungen zur Entstehung, Struktur und Rezeption* (Hamburg, 1984).

Turchin, Barbara: 'Robert Schumann's Song Cycles: The Cycle within the Song', *19th Century Music*, viii (1985), 236–43.

Voss, Egon: 'Robert Schumanns Sinfonie in g-Moll', *NZfM* cxxxiii (1972), 312–19.

Wasielewski, Wilhelm Joseph von: *Robert Schumann*, 2nd edn. (Dresden, 1869).

—— *Schumanniana* (Bonn, 1883).

Waters, Edward N.: 'In All Forms & For All Mediums: *Music Division Acquisitions*', *Quarterly Journal of the Library of Congress*, xxx (1973), 48–50.

Weingartner, Felix: *Die Symphonie nach Beethoven*, 3rd edn. (Leipzig, 1909).

—— *Ratschläge für Aufführungen Klassischer Symphonien*, 4th edn. (Wiesbaden, 1958).

Index